THEY WEAR WIGS IN HOLLYWOOD

Reflections of a Hair Loss Survivor

by
Andree Amarica

This book is printed in Canada.
Publisher, Andree Amarica, email: aamarica@gmail.com

Cover Art: Christian Simard

ISBN # 978-0-9947886-0-3
ISBN # 978-0-9947886-1-0
Library and Archives of Canada Act
This book is under the Legal Deposit of Publications Regulations

First printing, June 2015

Dedication

I dedicate this book to all women and men who secretly suffer from hair problems or any physical conditions and are too shy, too ashamed or held back by pride to come forward with their ailments in public or in private. I wrote these lines for all women and men who feel they do not fit in a world where physical appearance takes precedence over inner beauty.

I also dedicate this work to my amazingly beautiful Mother who had her own challenges to deal with throughout her entire life. Looking back in retrospect at her own experience, I feel deep compassion and empathy for her inner battles. She had been born for a mere eight months when her mother passed away. From that moment on, her destiny was sealed with emotional and physical instability. She had been born with great talents, beauty and wonderful skills. Unfortunately these great talents were never given a fertile and supportive ground in order to fully develop these abilities.

Last but not least I want to thank my amazing life partner, George, who has always stood by me and showered me with infinite support and encouragements to enable all my talents to grow and flourish.

Contents

Introduction

My mother tongue is French and I grew up immersed in that culture surrounded by a loving French family. I learned English in the early years of my life. The reason I chose to write this book in English is simple. When we compare French with English, we conclude that English is simpler in its syntax, grammar and the structure of phrases. During the time I taught French to English people, I often heard my students mention how difficult French was for them. Too many rules and challenges. That being said, I hope you will forgive my style with the language of Shakespeare.

I do not pretend to be an expert, a scientist or specialist with regard to hair loss and Alopecia. I am a visual artist who felt compelled to write about my experience with hair loss in order to extend a compassionate eye and understanding in the impact it has on relationships and emotions. This book is written from an authentic and genuine place within. I do not claim to have the answers to all problems or solutions to the dichotomies of our lives. This work is a simple attempt to shed light in certain areas of our individual and collective journey so that many of us can find our own truth and answers. When we decide to reveal a long kept secret to others, there comes with it a great sense of relief.

Alopecia Nervosa is an auto immune condition which triggers consistent hair loss and in extreme cases baldness. This condition is exacerbated when stress and anxiety permeate. This situation can affect our self-worth, self-doubt and self-identity. This book is filled with thousands of words like grains of sand on a huge beach in the attempt the best way possible, to describe what it is like to live a reality with physical challenges.

The events and circumstances described in this book have no specific linear or chronological order. For all of us who love the outdoors but experience physical restraints, whether scuba diving, snorkeling in the deep waters of the South Seas or skiing, our motto should be: "where there is a will there is a way".

I am excited to share my journey with you through these pages. I hope this information will help many people and alleviate the negative connotation associated with hair loss. I also hope that the reflections shared throughout this work will bring a ray of hope in the darkest places within each of us when confronted with any profound dilemma or impasse.

CHAPTER ONE

Body/Mind Connection

Suffering cannot be measured. The intensity varies for each individual. Life is lived behind closed doors. Suffering is vast on so many levels and degrees. Perceptions and attitudes play an important role in our individual processing. We cannot judge the book by its cover. We could take five people confronted with the same situation, and yet the processing and interpretation of that experience would be different for each one of them. Our perception and assessment of a given situation is based on our emotional, psychological and spiritual background we were born with and that emotional luggage we accumulate over the years can become unbearable. We are all complex individuals with our memories, our feelings, our joys, our scars and our disappointments. The question is what to do with this stored information?

How can we train ourselves to live happily with the good and the bad? It is worthwhile to look into these matters very carefully in order to find answers to these questions.

One important element we must look into is the powerful relationship we have established between our mind and our body. That relationship has a strong impact on shaping our whole being. That connection goes deep into the psyche of our lives as human beings and at the end of the day we are the end result of that delicate link between these two.

Each thought, emotion, and feeling we experience each day whether we are aware of them or not, have a direct effect on every single cell of our body as if each cell is a silent witness of all that happens to us. The cells are like little sponges soaking in every single minute detail and this, every second of one's existence without missing a beat, without us even knowing it.

These feelings and emotions have a tremendous impact on our body and the operating systems of each organ. There is a saying which mentions that "the outside reflects the inside and vice versa". If we carefully look at someone's face, we can observe whether that person has tendencies to worry or to be happy. If the person has deep lines on the forehead, it is easy to assume that it is due to worrying too much. It is like reading a road map. We cannot however, ignore the fact that we all begin our life with the body we are given at birth from our parent's genetic and DNA heritage. There are many variables that contribute to our physical health.

When the body lacks important nutrients or becomes loaded with toxins of all kinds, the mind experiences fogginess thus affecting our moods. The results can be devastating and can cause depression or apathy. The body impacts the mind and the activities of the mind will affect our physiology as well. One is dependent on the other. They operate hand in hand. It is as if we are artists in front a white canvas and we get to choose the colors, the shapes and the lines which at the end will be the final result from all these multiple choices.

This mind/body connection is the very foundation of our self-identity and self-worth. My father used to tell me that one is as old as one feels. It is independent from chronological age. You could be 20 and yet feel old or 80 and feel wonderfully young.

In order for me to elaborate better this topic of body/mind relationship, I will share with you a quote from one of my favorite authors, Doctor Deepak Chopra. In one of his books, he says "if we want to know what our thoughts and emotions were like ten years ago, we simply have to look at ourselves in the mirror today and we will know. If we want to know how we will look like ten years from now, all we have to do is take a good look at our thoughts and emotions we are experiencing in our lives now." (Ref. #1)

Here I want to highlight a concrete example of that relationship we have with our bodies and our mind.

I had a longtime friend whom I will call Laura. Laura passed away four years ago after battling for years with a lingering and painful cervical cancer at the age of forty three. She left behind her 12 year old son, friends and family. Laura had been born with great fortune on all levels. She had inner and outer beauty. I always admired her amazingly long shiny thick blonde hair. I also admired her smart savvy business sense as she had launched a successful internet company a few years back. She traveled all over the world. She was fearless. Laura practiced every sport from scuba diving, sky diving, white water rafting and snowboarding. Any given sports or activities that represented high adrenaline charge were hers to try. Laura had such inner strength and courage. It constantly amazed me how nothing stopped that girl! The sky was the limit for her. Anything was possible. She was the kind of person who loved life with passion. But little did we know that inside Laura's mind hid a deep, very deep secret filled with torment and anxiety. That deep hidden secret was chewing her zest for life, slowly but surely. She never shared that secret with anyone and kept going throughout her life as if nothing ever happened. Maybe that is why she was highly demanding with herself and had huge expectations. Thus why she also was a high risk taker.

Because we all know that nothing in life is permanent and because we know how devastating the effects of constant anxiety can have on the body, the story of Laura does not come as a surprise. A twist of circumstances and fate took an unexpected turn in Laura's life. Here is the fate she would have never wished for. We found out Laura had developed a cervical cancer.

CHAPTER TWO

The Passing of Laura

During a brutally cold winter day in January, the doorbell of our house rang and on the front steps stood my dear friend Laura shivering, looking so skinny and frail. With a feeble and vulnerable tone of voice she told me that she needed to talk to someone about something that was highly private. I could sense such despair and fear in her eyes. We sat on the floor of the living room by the fireplace. I looked at her in silence with compassion and noticed how fast her once beautiful and young body had quickly deteriorated. She had changed exponentially within just a few months. I was shocked and could see her emaciated facial features affected by the disease. I wanted to cry but held back my tears in order to focus on what she had come to tell me.

She expressed what she had endured for years carrying the burden of a secret without being allowed to tell anyone. Now, because of her cancer, she was ready to face the truth head on. She told me with genuine honesty that she felt a link between the hidden secret and the cancer. This was her honest interpretation of her reality. Not only had it been taxing on her body but also on her spirit which was starting to break down quickly. She was faced with too many changes all at once. As a mother, she knew she had to stay strong for her son.

Not only was she facing her past but she was also facing the gradual loss of her magnificent blond mane. She said that she had done some research online in order to find different options for hair loss. Every day she would wake up and find more missing patches of hair. She rejected the idea of wearing a full wig. In her opinion, wearing a wig would simply indicate a defeat in the face of the disease.

She then said she was planning a trip to the Caribbean to celebrate her twelve year old son's birthday. She wanted to go snorkeling and scuba diving against all odds. It was her first exposure to such a dire situation in dealing with hair issues. As I am sitting in front of her, listening to her dilemmas with hair loss, I had a moment of revelation, a "aha" moment. My discussion with Laura made me aware of the fact that all my life I had been confronted with uneasy situations because of Alopecia. It was a crucial moment and I realized that my own experience could serve in helping others with similar issues. Maybe my silent sufferance had not been in vain after all.

It was the first time ever that I decided to reveal my own secret with someone. Laura was stunned by that revelation and took a great interest and respect in what I had to offer technically and practically with hair issues. We deeply bonded after our confessions and became very close. An authenticity developed between us and our friendship took a quantum leap of growth.

In the following weeks after that deep connection we both shared, I began a routine where I would stop at her house, on my way back home to check on him. Her place was not even five minutes from my house. At first, she would come and open the door for me. After a while, her physical condition would not allow her to answer the door because of her increasing severe weakness. Under these circumstances, she had given me the permission to enter.

In general, when I entered her house, passing through the vestibule, I would find her laying on her couch looking like a lost child among the big piled pillows spread all around her thin and emaciated frame. Changes in her body were progressing ferociously. I would often notice tears dripping slowly down her cheeks as she would silently weep in even in my presence but no complaints. What impressed me the most was despite the excruciating pain she was in, she never said anything negative about her condition. She showed such courage in her determination and her will to heal. She did not give up and was still nurturing the hope that one day she would survive that cancer. She wanted to live and she wanted to be there for her son's graduation, to be a witness at his college graduation, to be there for his future wedding, and for all other important passages of his life. She loved him more than her own life.

One day, I was wondering why Laura had stopped calling me or sending me emails. It seemed that all lines of communications had shot down all at once. I got worried and stopped at her house as usual. To my surprise, there was no light, the TV was not on, no sign of life inside as I looked through the window and oddly enough, the door was locked. Stillness was permeating through the walls of her house. It was slightly creepy because it was as if the house had lost its own life. I rang and rang the bell to no avail. I felt a cold sweat going throughout my body and felt my blood going down to my toes all at once. I left the premises with a strange sensation in my heart and went back to my house.

Coincidently, as I stepped in the entrance way of our property, I heard the phone ring, I hastily ran inside and answered still with my coat on. It was our mutual dear friend Michael. Michael had been her most stable companion who showed absolute commitment toward her. Michael's voice was filled with emotion and sadness. He explained that the day before, Laura had been rushed urgently to the intensive care unit at the nearest hospital. Then, they had to send her to a palliative care unit since her life signs were almost gone.

A few hours later, she gave her last breath and passed away surrounded by him, along with close friends and her immediate family members. I silently wept as I carefully absorbed Michael's poignant rendition of her final moments. I had to say goodbye to my lovely girlfriend Laura whom had gone too young and too soon. She brought along with her a deep mysterious secret no one will ever know.

At this point, there was no need for me or anyone else for that matter to find out what exactly had happened to Laura. What had made her choose silence over deliverance? I had to accept all these facts all at once and make peace with it myself as I was letting go of her physical form like a delicate feather that was glued to a finger and was carried away by a strong wind.

I will always remember her beautiful angelic face and her gorgeous blond hair cascading down like a majestic river on her back. To this day I wonder if she had been aware of all the blessings and gifts that she had been given during her short life. One will never know but the important thing is that she has touched us all.

CHAPTER THREE

Beauty Defined Through Social Media

In many countries around the world and in various cultures, beauty and sexiness for women are often defined by hair. Young girls around the world identify themselves primarily by these attributes. Of all places, India is famous for the quality of hair women are donned with. The same applies for Middle Eastern countries and Asia. In fact there is a world trade where women will sell their hair to various businesses involved in the fabrication of wigs.

Since we live in a society where we give much importance to physical appearance, it can be detrimental and invalidating if any of the required physical characteristics our society demands are absent.

The increase in popularity and rapid growth with the social networks, in the last twelve years has exacerbated the focus on our physical requirements. The "I" seems to be predominant in a world where "I" phones, "I" pads, "I" Tunes, "My" space underline the importance of "I" "me" "my". The "I" is defined by how we look at ourselves and compare ourselves with others. We see more and more of so called "selfies". It is as if we are now at the center of a self-absorbed society filled with narcissism, obsessed with our navel and nothing pass that level. This could explain why it is tempting to fall prey into the traps of comparing each other on various levels.

The symptoms of comparative behavioral patterns are as such: one may begin to focus on the amazing performances of friends, their world travels, achievements and exciting lives they proudly provide to us daily in their profile. It is almost like a frantic race in keeping each other regularly updated with only fabulous aspects of our lives.

Sometimes it becomes quite obvious to conclude that one tries to outdo the other just like little kids do as if it were a wild race. Remember when we were little and our neighbor would say "Well my daddy is stronger than your daddy" and you would reply "Well my uncle is a police and he is more powerful than your daddy" or something similar. The difference is now we are adults and yet we still behave like kids.

I find it interesting to observe that many of us rarely share our inner demons, our fears and anxiety, our misery or sufferance on these networks. God forbid if one would dare, because it would be considered as politically incorrect and would shatter the perfect image we try so hard to project.

Instead of getting down to real business and call it for what it really is, we have a tendency, from time to time to inflate reality by posting only the best pictures and share the best situations. It appears that these social networks have created a larger than life inflated egomania. It created a monster of grandeur. We avoid like pest anything which relates to weakness, dysfunction, defects or weirdness of all kinds. We are creating a virtual world based on illusions.

I am not saying that all contents of these social networks present only negative patterns. We frequently hear about inspiring stories and testimonies which came from people who reached out with a specific dilemma to thousands of people via social media. These stories result in positive and creative aspects improving lives everywhere. We just need to use our good sense, our lucidity, and trust in our good individual judgment.

Statistics indicate that there has been an increasing number of people suffering with depression due partly to these networks. Studies also show that when people compare their own daily life with the lives of others who seem to have it better, the results can be detrimental to their happiness. There were several TV series on BBC called "The happiness formula". The series analyzed how people react when they notice that their neighbor has more than them. One example was that ten people sat in a room. Each was given one dollar and everybody was happy with that. The situation changed when one of these people was given ten dollars. All of a sudden the entire group dynamic changed from one minute to the next. The conclusion of one episode was that we as a society, when confronted by people who seem to have it bigger and better than us, there is an immediate alarm system switch that turns on. That switch is called threat. Needless to add that there is subsequently successive chain reactions due to that fear factor. This is how the rat race was born.

Let us go back to the social networks phenomena for a second. What frequently happens when people are dissatisfied with their own life, they will indulge in going into the profiles of their friends and compare notes with theirs. It is a form of voyeurism. Living one's life by procuration through the others.

It seems our reality at this time leaves very little space for the beauty which lies inside the "I". If only our eyes could see the soul behind the physical forms. That would transform our inter-relations. Our society is submerged and ruled by superficial values. These values result in an increased number of depressed people because the pressure on us is based on unreal expectations. These demands create a wide gap between the outer world and inner world. I hope for the sake of our collectivity this will not become the essential purpose of our humanity.

Another factor which contributes to quickly throwing our temporary happy little selves off is when while looking at ourselves in a mirror, we detect some physical changes in our body. Whether we find some hair missing here and there or some weight gain, sagging skin, or wrinkles to name a few, an immediate sense of panic flares up. These changes often will challenge us at the core of our self-esteem and identity. We become insecure, vulnerable and as a result, our sexual appeal gets shaken because we feel less attractive. Sexual appeal seems to have much power in how we define our identity.

It is also interesting to observe how we react in the presence of individuals who have physical anomalies. We experience discomfort and in general we will feel a bit uneasy. One reason could be that these anomalies do not fit with the standards of beauty we have set in a collective agreement. As a society we have a responsibility to ask ourselves why we have these reactions. Could it be that we have been conditioned to automatically reject and condemn anything that stands out as an eye sore in the ocean of homogeneity? It is apparent that when our stereotypes of beauty fail, so does our good judgment.

Maybe this is why we feel safer living in homogeneity where similitude prevails instead of standing high and strong with pride with what we have been given inside and outside. There are now over six billions human beings on our planet and yet not one single body looks the same. Even identical twins will show disparities. Have you ever sit by yourself in a coffee shop and indulged in doing what I call "people watching"? If so, you must have quickly concluded that in these short ten minutes, you saw an infinite number of differences in these bodies. Fascinating isn't it?

Because of this infinite variety of bodies, we do not have a choice but train ourselves in learning how to live with our differences. Showing a little more compassion, tolerance and understanding certainly will not hurt anyone. It would make our lives much richer if we could openly share our emotional and physical stigmas without fear or restraint. By doing so, we would be able to heal collectively and evolve in a more constructive way. Knowing that we are not alone in our predicaments sometimes can be so encouraging and can save many lives.

Let us get real about the ideal of beauty and the infinite pursuit of physical perfection. It is an inaccessible dream which is not based on true facts. We must keep in mind that glossy magazines and advertisement use airbrushing technology. This only reinforces the illusion of perfection. We erase all evidence of aging signs, excess of bulges and fat, erasing with that all sense of what is real and unreal. It is as if these features were some kind of disease to be avoided at any cost.

A new mentality is born and shows zero tolerance for flaws. Criticisms are out of control. Harsh comments are made on any public figures. We no longer listen to what writers, actors, journalists or singers have to say but more how they look like and what they wear. Any red carpet event is a good example. The dresses women wear take precedence over the role they played in any movies. Not only do we all have to look forever young, pretty or dashingly handsome, we also have to look very happy as if we never have any problems or obstacles. Oh and let's not forget we all have to display the whitest and brightest smile possible.

One thing I realized in the last few years is that the only real competition we face at the end of the day is with our own self. We can become our own worst enemy and worse harsh critic.

We have to make peace with these areas and develop detachment and even humor toward the many changes we all face often too soon than later. The laws of nature on the physical plane are such that wear and tear is inevitable for all living creatures. Nobody is spared. All humans and all wild life are bound to undergo changes such as transformation, decay and death. These are certainties none of us can avoid. Even the largest celestial bodies such as stars, planets and suns eventually die. The sooner we come to terms with the fact that all lives are temporary, the better it will be for our own salvation. As a consequence, we will bring in light and empowerment in ourselves with more stability. Safety has to come from within first and foremost. Safety comes from handling and developing values that are based on essential elements for the sake of our well-being. Instead of being constantly obsessed with our bodies which only lasts a life time, whatever time is given to each of us, why not focus primarily on our inner growth. There is not a specific age to die but only an hour, meaning that when our time is up this is it. There is a beautiful saying which goes as follows: "when our time is not up, no army can kill us and when our time is up, no army can save us".

We have to start looking at ourselves with our own eyes and not with the eyes of social media for that matter. We also have to find our own meaning to the word "success" and what significance it has for us. Could it be that true success is a feeling contentment and inner happiness, independent of what the outside offers? What do we succeed exactly? Success of what? It is up to you and me to answer these fundamental questions. There will be as many answers as there are as many beings and many layers in one's life. One person can be successful with money and another one with friendships and another one with a career. These successes are compartments in the whole of one's life. It is as if we define our life as a chest of drawers. One drawer is for our friends, another one for our social activities, another for our career and yet another one for our financial gains. These drawers as full as they can get will not necessarily guarantee happiness and fulfillment.

Dr Tony Nader wrote in his book "Human Physiology"; "The ever-expanding universe is an always-changing, never-the-same, field of dynamism... Nothing in this relative, physical manifested world remains the same. The only consistency is "change"... (see references)

In other words, it is for our own benefit if we realize that permanence comes from within. We must make peace with change as soon as possible and let go of resistance. That is a big step forward in the achievement of inner happiness.

CHAPTER FOUR

Heredity

One morning, when I was about three years old, I remember sitting at the kitchen table drinking a glass of milk and playing with my golden curls, which were gently touching the sides of my baby face. I felt a sense of pride with my long golden hair. My mother was standing beside me holding a brush. Our daily ritual was the same every day. While I sat there she would gently comb my hair. It was, I guess a mother and child bonding moment. All of a sudden one day, she screamed with horror. She said out loud: "Oh my God, my child is losing so much hair"!

Following that painful morning, my mother promptly brought me to her hair salon to chop off most of my hair. When I looked at myself in the mirror, I was a three year old girl looking like a boy ready to join the army. Devastation and a sense of loss overwhelmed my little person. My short lived pride with my blond gold locks had just been terminated. This crucial moment gave birth to a love/hate relationship with my hair. Little did my mother know that the problem could not be solved just with a haircut. She had never been exposed to various hair loss problems such as alopecia nervosa.

Being so young and having to deal with these physical issues can be highly taxing on one' self-esteem. Hair issues are especially important for a girl growing from childhood to adolescence. Much attention is given to it more for girls than boys.

Capillary issues such as what makes hair thick or thin are delicate. We have to consider many factors. First, the proper nutrients needed for the child's normal development are essential. Secondly, we have to keep in mind that the genetic heritage plays an important part in the physiological make up. In my case, my mother had been diligent with the quality of our food intakes. She made sure that we had the right amounts of vitamins and minerals. That aspect of our life was well balanced. Unfortunately, my genetic heritage came from countries where it is typical to have very frizzy and thin hair. It came from the pool of Irish, Scottish, and French genes on my father's side and on my mother's side I had native Indian and Slavic blood.

All of my father's sisters had baby fine frizzy blond hair which resembled more like Velcro or the chia dog.

On my mother's side however, all of her sisters had beautiful thick shiny straight strawberry blond hair. The luck of the draw was in my case the Scottish side won the genetic war. I was aware that my situation was not the worse in comparison to so many kids from different parts of the world who suffer the worst conditions, from missing limbs to straight hunger and malnutrition.

The truth of the matter is that when you are very young and at the start of your life and you do not know better or worse, reality is very limited in that young little person's perceptions. Living in North America also may hinder our judgment. It is like rolling the dice and see what results will come out.

Various studies in the fields of psychology confirm that self-esteem and self-image are determined during the ages of zero and twelve. In my case, the first challenge happened at age three. The relationship I had with my mother was mostly always related to my hair. She indirectly enabled my growing hatred toward any aspects of my body. Whether it was my hair, my thinness or my breasts size. I could never meet her standards.

She focused on the aspects of my body that did not fit her expectations. She scrutinized and criticized me too often. My mother grew up in a family where boys were adulated. This family situation made her doubt herself and made her question her own self-identity. She subconsciously passed them on to me by osmosis. When time came to wash my hair, it was an ordeal for both of us. My mother constantly battled with my frizzy hair in such a way that she would pull my curls so hard as if she was exorcizing her own frustrations on my head. I have to laugh today when I look back at this scenario because I know it was a therapy for her. However, for a little three year old girl, the impact is dramatic, to say the least.

As the years went by, the focus put on capillary issues intensified. I blamed the fragility and insecurity I felt inside because of my hair. When in class, during my early teen years, I often indulged in looking at all the girls' hair and compare myself with them. I was overwhelmed by how many girls were endowed with magnificent long straight hair or thick wavy styles whether blond, brown or black manes. They seemed to take for granted that they were given such a precious commodity that I could only dream of, in silence.

One day after a typical day at school, I came home with an idea. I went in my mother's drawers and found this beautiful long brown silk scarf. I creatively folded it in two, took bobby pins and then put it on in such a way that each side of my head looked as if I had long silky straight brown hair. It made me feel happy for a short moment. I would go around my room, shaking my head and feel the bounce and the softness of it on both sides of my face. In my fertile imagination, it was real hair. That was my own little secret behind the doors of my little pink bedroom. This scenario became part of my daily life, after school. I would go on pretending I was a famous French actress wearing different hair styles and different colors. I had developed my own creative strategy in handling my deplorable hair condition. An imaginary star was born.

CHAPTER FIVE

The Loss of My Only Sister

I only had one sister who was fourteen years my senior. She left home when I was six years old. She had applied for a job as a flight attendant with a major airline company. She was hired and moved away to New York City. When she left home, I experienced a profound sadness and a deep sense of loss. In my eyes, she represented the ideal of feminine beauty. I had such admiration for her on all levels.

My big sister also played the role of a second mother since my own mother had me when she was forty. She had raised the family and felt tired most of the time with my tough adolescence. I was the baby of the family. My sister had all the qualities that could be defined as physical ideal. She was tall, slim, with fine facial features and big deep blue eyes like the ocean. She also had inherited the genes of our Irish and Scottish background meaning frizzy hair.

Every time she came back home for a visit, it was party time. Whenever my mother came up with the good news that my sister was coming for a week, I would jump up and down with joy. We shared my bedroom. Prior to going out for dinner, she would get ready by putting make up and choose her outfit. I would stand beside her, carefully watching every move. I would focus on how she applied her make up. In my eyes, she was the most beautiful woman in the world, as gorgeous as an angel or as a Hollywood or French actress. Actually, all our male neighbors, would secretly behind their doors watch her walking from church. I caught a few wondering eyes one day and felt great pride.

The fact that my sister lived in a big cosmopolitan city such as New York City, helped her with the discovery of revolutionary techniques for straightening curly hair. She used to be a regular customer at the Vidal Sassoon salons. Some treatments involved hair products that had loads of heavy toxic chemicals while others were creams you would apply before blow drying. She taught me these secrets and from that moment on I gained a certain assurance and confidence about my looks. The joy was always short lived because my hair reacted to high humidity and rain. What a frustration it always was. Imagine that after spending almost an hour trying to straighten the curls on a humid day, it would take only one minute spent outside to bring back the frizzy curls. Curls that looked like some wild bouncing springs of a bed mattress.

This battle went on for days, weeks and months. I had no choice but learn how to deal with this reality and come to terms with my frizzy fate. I kept repeating myself that life could be worse. This fact complicated my life as a young girl because I loved the outdoor sports so much. I liked skiing, horseback riding and swimming. But as we know most of these sports require carefree hair concerns.

I decided to take the bull by the horns as my big sister would tell me and proceeded to be bigger than that limitation. I was well aware that somewhere in other countries in the world, there were young girls my age who had to face terrible serious stigmas. I felt embarrassment in putting such emphasis with a simple hair problem of Alopecia.

When we hear about these poor girls in some parts of the world who get attacked with acid thrown on their faces because they crave for independence. These girls get disfigured by these criminal acts for the sake of claiming their freedom. Here I was taking so many things in my life for granted. Despite the fact that I was aware of these incidents, my reality was the only one I was dealing with. I was trying to cope in the best way that I could with the means I was given at the time.

I decided to expand my fields of interests. I started devouring books on psychology and parapsychology. Revelations and breakthroughs helped me understand different given human conditions. My priorities were slowly and gradually shifting as a young adult and took more of a vertical direction rather than a horizontal one. To this day I am grateful to life that I shifted my reality to a deeper and more meaningful existence because in retrospect, I was getting ready to go through one of the most difficult events that anyone can imagine, the loss of my big sister.

On a dark, cold March evening, my husband and I were driving back from Montreal. The two hour drive had been filled with stress and nervousness because of bad road conditions. Upon entering the house, for no reason, my heart started beating fast and I started experiencing a rather strange uneasiness. My phone was flashing indicating I had a voicemail. I picked up the phone and before listening to the message, I intuitively knew it was not good news. I felt it was probably my father since he was getting there in age. Little did I know that it would be the worst nightmare of losses. My beloved sister had been killed in a car crash upstate New York on a small windy country road at four o'clock that afternoon. She and her husband were getting their dining room ready to welcome their first guests in their Country Inn. She had run out of paint and decided to go get some more at the hardware store which was a thirty minute drive from their place. That day, light snow had fallen and had covered the roads with a thin white carpet. Black ice became invisible to the eye.

According to the reports, the accident occurred in the worse curves of highway 42. It was a fatal head on collision. I remember how that news felt in every cell of my being. The silence in the house was so thick and so loud to my ears that I could have cut it with a knife. I felt my blood was being sucked out of my entire body. It felt as if the earth beneath my feet was cracked open. I grabbed her picture and stared at it knowing perfectly well that this was the end of a wonderful and glamorous life she had. The worst thing was being aware I would never get to see that lovely face ever again except in photographs. It was like a shattered mirror falling in thousands of pieces like snowflakes in slow motion on a cold marble floor. The impact of the broken glass felt like eternity.

The strange thing is that four days prior to her fatal accident, we had been playing phone tags. Finally the day before she died, we luckily connected. She said something rather unusual. She asked me if I would like to come to New York and be with her so that I could help her putting order with her wardrobe. She said she needed to get rid of stuff in order to simplify her life. She told me the best time for me to come would be in the beginning of March more or less after our mother's birthday which was March 4th. I replied positively with enthusiasm. At that time, I had started my own little fashion consulting business. Before our phone conversation ended, I told her how much I loved her and admired her. Strangely, she remained silent on the other end, which was totally out of character for her. She had always showed joy, love, passion and a zest for life. I felt something I had never experienced before in my relationship with my sister. I do not want to mystify this experience but that last phone conversation felt as if a huge cosmic bridge, a bridge larger than life had been put between us within hours only. Were these signs or premonitions of ominous circumstances that were yet to come?

She died the day after my mother's birthday, March 5th. Her death made me realize how transient our existence is and how it can shift and change radically from one second to the next. Her loss helped me put my problems in proper perspective. What was important to me before this tragedy suddenly appeared trivial? I clearly understood that we cannot take what and who we have in our lives for granted because it is all temporary. We must focus on what is essential in our day to day living. We must tell our dear ones how we feel, without being afraid to express our love to them. At the end of the day this is what we will leave behind. The love we gave one another, the people we helped and the ones we held and supported, this will be the ultimate legacy. At least, I had no residual regrets with her passing since I had always expressed my tendering love and affection for her and this, to the end.

Our way of connecting today in our digital reality is mostly virtual. Emailing, texting, tweeting are our method of communication. Soon, the telephone will become archaic. We are so busy with our activities that more often than not we forget to really connect with candor. It is a sad state of affairs for many of us. As a result, isolation and loneliness are growing in big cities with tragic outcomes. This will impact many generations to come.

We must not wait for someone to die in order to reach out to each other. The death of my sister helped me experience what I would call a "spiritual quantum leap". Needless to say that from that moment on, my life radically changed. When events such as death happen, one can only feel humility toward the vastness of our universe we live in. Our understanding of things is limited by our materialistic vision of reality. As a Western society we have a tendency to shun with great aversion such words like death, ageing, and handicap.

My sister's death shook me and woke me up like a hammer on the head. It brought me from a state of constant pursuit of pleasure to a place where all was revealed in truth. It reminds me of a quote I always cherished. It is from a book I read hundreds of time when I was a child. It is "The Little Prince" of Saint-Exupery. The excerpt is following the moment where the little prince fell in love with a rose and thought it was unique. He then becomes aware there are thousands of roses which just look the same. He is devastated by that observation. The fox sees how disappointed the Little Prince is and says to him:-"Your rose is unique. We only see through the heart because the essential is invisible to the eyes". This tragic loss of my dear sister made me understand this beautiful quote. From that moment on, I desperately was on a quest for something deeper, stronger and more permanent within.

CHAPTER SIX

The Initiation

One day after school, my big brother, whom at that time was an art professor at a university, told me about a lecture he was going to attend. The subject of the lecture was meditation. He recommended that I join him. I went and am glad I did. The lecturer exuded calmness and serenity. He radiated health and bliss. The presentation addressed issues of growth and prosperity through the experience of inner relaxation of the mind and body. He talked about our amazing mental potential and abilities that often remain dormant. By the stimulation of certain parts of the brain, one could enhance brain power with the help of powerful techniques such as meditation. He also mentioned that during the normal course of a human life, one might only use 6 to 10% of mental potential. All these elements and facts resonated positively with me.

I began to practice that technique and immediately saw concrete results. My life started changing in a more positive way. My marks at school scored higher than ever. I did not seem to put more effort in my studies but the results were astonishing. I was growing quickly, leaving behind my dark teenage years. I was becoming a young adult ready to face the world with all good things in my light suitcase of life. A new promising decade and a new vision were waiting for me at the dawn of a new horizon.

I became aware that I had to take responsibility for all aspects of my existence and that meant taking charge of my hair challenges as well. Believe me I am very aware it sounds funny. The healthy way of handling the hair situation was simply by enhancing the content of my life with more redeeming values as opposed to identifying myself with shallow problems. How silly it had been to spend so much of my precious energy on hair. Whether the hair was too curly, too short, too thin or too long I progressively developed a healthy detachment. It was a beautiful growth in my awareness. I started functioning from a deeper level of existence by switching my attention into what was essential. The obsession with physical appearance gave way to spiritual values.

One day, I had to apply for a job that represented everything to me. I had dreamed of that type of work forever. It had to do with journalism. I had to travel throughout Canada and interview heads of companies who wanted to go on an international level and write about it.

The job application quickly put me back in the reality of living in a body. I was aware that during job interviews, physical appearance plays an important role. Apparently it takes only four minutes for the interviewer to decide on the candidate. In these first few minutes, one is not necessarily judged for the academic credentials but rather on the physical impression.

Four days after the interview, I was asked to come back for a last and final interview. It is during that meeting that I found out I had been selected among 15 other candidates for the position. I was puzzled with the results since the other candidates had more credentials than I did. However needless to say I felt elated.

Many months later, while I was doing a search for my work tasks, I got a hold of my private file and found out that I had been chosen not necessarily for my mental abilities and credentials but for the way I looked. I was quite surprised by that report. My hair at the time was thick with beautiful curls. It created a sweet romantic look and softened the edges of my oval face. After finding out about the content of the file, I started questioning professional integrity as well as professional ethics. I had so many unanswered questions.

From childhood to adulthood we all face experiences which will make us feel on top of our game or feel like we do not belong. This is called the law of the fittest. The survival game of the rat race that is typical in our modern society. The intellectual and mental abilities of an individual are often secondary to the physical appearance. Research has showed that physical attractiveness enables more success and good fortune.   In many fields of the work force, handsome people will make more money per year than others. Babies who are cute will draw more attention than their less fortunate counterparts. It appears that reality in this world is based on "appearance".

CHAPTER SEVEN

The Challenges of Alopecia

There were certain periods of my life where the hair issue was put to sleep. I would have phases where all events, circumstances and experiences in my life were smooth and empowering. I had good friends and my family was a loving one. I was happy in my relationship with my husband who thought I looked as if I was out of a Vogue magazine. Of course, I did not believe him because he was my husband. His compliments were so refreshing to me because during my teenage years, the boyfriends I dated, had the tendencies to put me down in one way or another. Interestingly enough I grew up believing that these comments were the absolute truth.

I always thought that boys were attracted to me because of my inquisitive mind and not for my physical appearance. My interests grew more toward philosophy, history and cosmogony. I was passionate about quantum physics and the structure of our universe from the microcosm to the macrocosm. I guess that impressed the boys. My husband was the first man I ever met who found me pretty. He also respected my intellectual curiosity and hunger for knowledge.

It was a hot day in the month of July when my husband and I decided to go out for a boat ride on a lake. We decided to bring with us a lovely picnic. When we arrived on the small island off the shore of the lake, one of our friends was already there by the beach. He looked at me in an inquisitive way as if he was some kind of fashion editor/photographer. After a long pause, he suggested I join a modeling agency because he felt I could make money as a model.

Three days after that beautiful warm summer day, I followed up with his suggestion and called an agent to book an interview with the director. I arrived to my appointment ten minutes ahead of time to be more relaxed and at ease. I observed with focus the decoration of the place. It was tastefully done in modern minimalist designs. I saw photographs of models hanging on every wall. Obviously these models were represented by this agency. All these girls looked so beautiful and glamorous. I felt that maybe I was not supposed to be here for the reason I had intended. Suddenly I heard footsteps coming from the large corridor. These steps covered a silence so still that I thought no one was there but me. In the door frame, a tall beautiful woman appeared. Her face was chiseled with amazingly perfect features. Her hair sat like a crown on her head. Thick wavy dark brown mane falling gracefully slightly above the shoulders. She introduced herself as the owner of the modeling agency and the general director.

She scrutinized every square inch of my appearance, from head to toe. After a very long and boring scrutiny she announced that they would take me on a trial basis. The world of modeling was a strange new land in my eyes. That world seemed to collide in extreme opposition with my philosophy of life. Little did I know what was ahead for me?

I left her office feeling happy and quite detached from the outcome. Shortly after, many contracts came my way. I felt puzzled with these contracts because they were all for similar products in nature. They rotated around promotional campaigns for new lines of bathing suits or for yoga apparels. I did not like the feeling of my photo sessions because the technicians and photographers were all men. This represented a serious challenge for me since I had always been dealing with body issues, like most women. I did not enjoy the castings either because in my eyes, we were treated like we were part of some cattle. We would be on a stage while the jury, mostly men sitting not even five feet from us, would judge who would be rejected and who would stay. All of us girls were there trying to sell our goods (which is exactly what it was). That part will never be part of my fondest memories in my short-lived career as a model. On the other hand, the fact was I was making good money and I certainly could not complain about that aspect.

One evening, after a photo shoot, the director of the agency requested a private meeting with me. We sat in her big sterile office while her assistant was taking notes. She was whispering softly on the phone with a client. I was unable to hear the words. While waiting, I turned my head toward the ceiling. The room reminded me of some living room one would find in a gothic castle somewhere in England. The high cathedral ceilings made this place cold and unwelcoming. The words 'quaint" and 'cozy' would definitely not be part of the description of that office. She finally ended her telephone discussion and had a big sigh. She stared at me without a word for a minute (which felt like an eternity). Finally she started a dialogue with me. Unfortunately for me, she did not begin the meeting by expressing positive feedbacks on all the work I had done. That would have been too much effort of diplomacy on her part. No, instead, she chose to adopt the aggressive pit-bull mode of operation. She bluntly asked me why on earth my hair was so frizzy. She went on and on incessantly coming back to why my hair was the way it was. In her opinion, my hair was not a good representation of the image the agency portrayed. Their image was sleek, minimalist but highly aesthetic. She continued by saying that if this situation was not promptly remedied, they would no longer offer me contracts. I stopped breathing for a second and felt my blood going one way to my toes. It was like a dagger thrown straight in my heart. I took a deep breath before reacting verbally. I replied that I would do the best I could in order to change that. It is interesting for me to remember this incidence because today I would have had a complete different take on this whole ridiculous scenario.

The challenge was immense. My hair dilemma came back and this time with torrential ripple effects. Night after night, I would have a stressful battle with the frizziness in order to prepare for my next day photo shoot. It was pure stress built up and all because of having hair issues that were hard to handle naturally. I tried every single given tools and formulas available at that time. Nothing seemed to work and if it did it was for maybe an hour or less.

I now vividly recall one day where I had a scheduled photo shoot. I presented myself on time and low and behold I found another model replacing me. I was told that her hair suited better for what was required from their client. Needless to say, I left the premises like a lightning bolt in complete shock and disbelief.

Next morning, over a cup of coffee, I reflected on this chapter of my life. I concluded it was complete insanity and waste of precious life to constantly expose myself to disempowering and invalidating situations. That moment represented a victory and a quantum leap in my individual understanding of things. I got in my car and sang at the top of my lungs "We are the champions" from the famous band "Queen". That was the end of my short-lived modeling career. Had I known myself better at the time, with a better sense of discrimination, I would have totally bypassed that entire episode of my life. I guess that is the beauty that comes from the acquired wisdom from life experience. It gives us back our own truth and our own voice.

One year later, my husband started his own company as an engineer and consultant for non-governmental agencies, for Foreign Affairs and the Canadian International Development Agency (CIDA). The type of work he was involved with demanded much travelling around the world. I was working full time as a writer for the city where we lived. I hated my job and felt quite out of place there. I jumped on the opportunity when my husband asked if I wanted to join his company as an administrative assistant. I said yes. Not only did I have the best boss but I got to travel all over the world with him.

The first few trips we took were easy with regard to quick and efficient beauty routines. I kept it minimal and simple.

However, that simple beauty ritual changed when alopecia came back more aggressive than ever. The stress of our travels did not help. I desperately read, searched for quick fixes and alternative remedies. I tried acupuncture, herbs, Chinese medicine etc... Nothing really helped or if it did, it was short lived. I decided to do serious research for possible good solutions. I discovered a hair magazine which gave good advice with different tips regarding hair problems of any kinds. They offered techniques on how one could get fuller looking hair. It mentioned how actresses and actors throughout the world took recourse in these alternatives. There were pictures of hair extensions, weaves, hair clips and full wigs. It drew my attention and I saw a light at the end of the tunnel. It gave me hope and we know hope is the best remedy. The events that followed were almost like part of a script written especially for my role.

One evening, on my way to a kick boxing class with my best girlfriend Maureen we stopped at her favorite hair accessory store. To my amazement, as we walked in, I discovered a whole parallel universe. It was called the world of hair enhancement. I felt like a kid walking into a candy store. Entire shelves filled with hair accessories, false pony tails, hair extension clips and wigs, tons of them, of all shapes, lengths, colors and textures. That place left me almost in a state of shock. Needless to say that I walked out with a bag full of goodies. When I arrived home, I displayed my purchases carefully on the bed and tried every single item. There they were laying on the bed, my newfound friends who would be my companions from now on. This was a moment I will not forget. I was about to live with a full head of hair again.

Every day after my shower, I would proceed to get dressed and just simply put on a clip which would fill the gap between the front and middle of the head. It made me look like I had amazing hair. As the months went by, I continued losing hair. For any women in their early 30's that could be alarming.

Alopecia can be aggressive in its progress or very slow in its devastation. In my case, it was an uneven slow torture. The Alopecia monster would go dormant for months and made me believe it was finally over once and for all. Until one day the monster would resurface. Some mornings, I would find so much hair on my pillow that I felt like a shedding dog in the spring time.

This problem caused much grief and high anxiety. I was caught in a vicious cycle. The cycle is that when we realize how much hair we lose, the more stressed we become and with the increase of stress comes more hair loss. I always preferred simplicity with my life. This problem was a big obstacle to that simple life. I got fed up and took the yellow pages determined to find an expert in the field of hair loss. Someone who would be able to guide me in a healthy yet easy direction. One day my prayers got answered. I met my angel monsieur Edouard.

CHAPTER EIGHT

My Dear Friend, Monsieur Edouard

This following experience is part of my fondest memories in relation to my hair problem. It was early December, one of the coldest weekends ever, for that time of year. I drove down to Montreal to meet with Monsieur Edouard for the first time. We had set up an appointment over the phone a week earlier. He insisted that we call him Monsieur Edouard and nothing else.

His name was Edouard Boulanger. He was a short sturdy man from Lac St-Jean. He displayed much eccentricity by the way he was dressed and how he had decorated the interior of his hair salon. His deep blue eyes were filled with depth and passionate intensity. Striking gaze like fire and ice.

His shop was a mirror image of himself. There were mannequins displayed everywhere wearing Venetian masks and wigs. There were statues of naked Apollos and beautiful glass sculptures hanging from the ceilings. And of course, there were heads of plaster wearing hats or sunglasses. I felt I had just walked in a Tim Burton movie or in Alibaba's cave filled with mystery and magic. Let's say it did not feel like a typical hair salon. The interior of the salon felt more like if we had been invited to some underground ceremony from a secret society. His employees were all more eccentric looking than the other. They looked like they were part of a travelling group of a Gypsy band. One girl displayed hair so orange that oranges would be jealous. Another person had a spandex Lycra outfit worth of any good contortionists from Le Cirque du Soleil.

It was late on Saturday afternoon when I arrived and the personnel was busy packing up and call it a day. Monsieur Edouard welcomed me in his salon with warmth and playfulness. He grabbed my right hand and twirled me around in the middle of the lobby like we were rehearsing for the show "Dancing with the stars". He asked me if I was a ballerina with Les Grands Ballets Canadiens because he thought I walked like one. I replied that I had learnt classical ballet from the age 7 to 16 then pursued in modern ballet for another five years. I still had this intense passion for dance in general.

Monsieur Edouard immediately conquered my fascination. I always felt drawn to eccentricity and he definitely did not fit in any typical box of normality. In my opinion, true original people do not have to try to be different. I suspect monsieur Edouard probably was born in a pool of eccentricity the first day he came into this world. That is what he told me as a joke. Original people are spontaneous in their approach to life in general and bring such a colorful edge in a world where grey and drab often dominate.

Monsieur Edouard's life story is so out of the ordinary. Here is a sliver of his mysterious life. He was a man who had been in the hair industry for over thirty years. He had started at a very young age back in Lac St-Jean as an assistant in the local hair salon in a small country village. He moved to the big metropolis of Montreal in his early twenties. He opened his first hair salon in the posh elitist neighborhood of Westmount where the wealthy and high society lived. He became very wealthy. His reputation became larger than life throughout various circles. Among his clients were many famous directors from the movie business and theatre. In the eighty's and ninety's, Montreal had hundreds of movie sets. For many American film companies, Montreal was the first place of choice to do movies because of low production costs and the Canadian dollar at the time was lower than its counterpart, the American dollar. There was a big margin between the two. Monsieur Edouard became a major supplier for all the actors and comedians who were in theatre plays and movies. The wigs, the hair extensions, the props all came from Monsieur Edouard's company. He lived up to his excellent reputation for a very long time. He worked hard and to his own detriment played hard too. He made big money and spent big too.

This was at a time where discos were at their height of popularity. Studio 54 in New York City and the Limelight in Montreal. Wherever Monsieur Edouard went, he had his entourage following him, like or Rock star. He lived that era to the fullest. His favorite motto was "life is short", let's live it up and that he did indeed. This was before the AIDS epidemic broke out.

This is his story he shared with me on the first few times I had ever met him and he told the story with impeccable details. I could just picture his tales as if I was watching a movie. Sadly enough when I met him much water had already run under the bridge of his life to this point. As the story goes, he woke up one morning filled with a deep emptiness inside. He looked around his big mansion all alone assessing his material gains he had acquired over the years. He had a great passion for antiques, especially wooden angels from various centuries. The house was located at the top of the mountain overlooking Mount Royal with a breathtaking view of the city. How strange it was to feel so empty inside when his outside life was full. Full of fancy cars, designer clothes and impressive collections of antiques. He always surrounded himself with such high profile characters. He was never physically alone and yet deep loneliness filled his heart.

He decided upon this observation that it was time for him to undertake a new project which would lead him to feel more fulfilled and useful as a human being. He felt he could do much more to contribute in helping others and leave a nice legacy behind. He decided to add a new division to his prolific business with a different mandate.

Monsieur Edouard created a project that would focus on people who were not gorgeous, rich nor famous. The mandate was going to be based on serving people who suffered from cancer and therefore dealing with hair loss and other ailments attached to hair loss. He would provide these people with a vast supply of hair pieces, wigs, hair extensions. We all know friends of family members who have undergone chemotherapy or other illnesses. It rubs off much dignity in the lives of too many people.

Monsieur Edouard's sincere commitment to this new venture impressed me. This project would succeed in putting a smile on people's faces again, giving them hope and make them feel alive again, despite what they were going through. That is what inspired me the most about him. I developed not only a business relation with him but also a profound friendship based on truth. The truth of each other's soul. No fancy pretexts and no phoniness.

I never had to explain myself to him. He quickly captured and understood who I really was and where I was coming from. He could duplicate his reality with mine and empathize with the challenges and dilemmas I had gone through because of my hair heritage. He was there to help me go through these existing challenges with positive solutions and strong encouraging coaching.

I visited Monsieur Edouard every time I drove to Montreal, not necessarily for new hair pieces or adjustments needed but to simply pay him a visit as a dear friend. We had developed a beautiful and nurturing friendship over these years. He would regularly check on me as I did with him. Sometimes I would come home worried about some of his personal choices and activities. He was walking on a fine thin edge most of the time. That edge brought some issues between us which from time to time were unpleasant to deal with.

Sadly enough, after a while, he developed a strong dependency on drugs and alcohol. We are talking about here an extreme degree of dependency. I rapidly saw a degeneration in his body. His lifestyle became highly taxing on his health. During every visit, I would discover a new progressive consequence from his dependencies. These habits do not come cheap as we know. They brought up some issues between us which, from time to time, were unpleasant to deal with. He needed money lots of it in order to support these habits. He basically lost everything, slowly but surely. I was a silent witness to this, step by step. The losses started with properties, then the cars, then the clothes, paintings and antiques were taken away as payments to his impending debts. Then tragically, his dear friends left him, one by one, just pulling away and disconnecting completely from him. His devoted employees became concerned and questioned his habits. It was so sad to see someone with such a great and kind heart go down at a rapid pace into the dwindling spiral of loneliness and self-destruction.

Despite his addictions, he still was able to create magnificent human hair pieces for me and I would go home so grateful. I was worried for him and wanted to help him so much. One day, he told me that he had been diagnosed with diabetes. His doctor obviously recommended that he should stop drinking but this advice was useless. It was at that very moment that I deeply felt he had given up and had thrown the towel on his life. I could see through his once clear deep blue eyes, a weariness and deep profound fatigue with life in general. He no longer had the strength to fight for anything anymore.

During one of my visits with him, I just had returned from a long journey to Europe. When he found out I had started painting abstract art during my stay over there, he immediately involved his time in marketing my work. He used all his contacts and connections in the artistic community of Montreal as well as in the music and theatre industry. I was touched by his support of my talents even if he was in a severe depression. I could feel that our allegiance gave him a sweet sparkle of hope in his heart. It moved me to see that. He asked me to stay for dinner that evening. We cooked together a tasty Italian meal and cracked jokes. We sat outside on his large terrace and watched the sparkling lights shining in the city like diamonds on a black sea. When it was time for me to drive back home, it was late and we hugged each other for what would be the last one ever.

He died at 60, fat, heart broken by all the deaths of his friends with AIDS and the loss of everything he had worked so hard for during his life. The most amazing thing is that a few days after my visit, just hours before he passed away, he left me a voice message at 3:00 pm. He had a faint and fragile tone of voice, asking me to call him as soon as I could. I tried and tried and two weeks went by. I never got the chance to speak with him ever again.

One day, after another try in calling him, out of the blue a male voice picked up the phone. He introduced himself as being Monsieur Edouard's brother. He told me that monsieur Edouard had died two hours after he had left his message in my voicemail. I can say with honesty that to this day he is one of my guardian angels, looking after me. He was a rare beautiful human being who cared for hair issues at large because he knew that at a deeper level, this fact was affecting other layers of our lives. Because of him I now have acquired ways to creatively cope with hair loss in a productive manner. So much so, that now, I never feel any less happy or inadequate with that issue. This has been his gift to me, his legacy will forever live in my heart and my hope is to convey this with many others.

To this day, I carry with me a lucky charm he once gave me. It broke in half but still it looks so special and I feel his presence through this object. After his passing away, I hoped that someone like him would come my way again to help me with creating beautiful hair pieces the same way he did, with compassion and support. These two emotions are so important in the lives of those who deal with hair loss, whether they are the ones who create these wigs or the ones who will eventually buy them. When one has Alopecia or other hair ailments, the wigs they acquire are not for trendy, short lived fashion statements but rather represent hope. These accessories allow us to fit in the world with dignity.

My dear friend had captured the very essence of that business. The nature of that business is similar to those companies who are major suppliers in the fabrication of prosthetic limbs, knee supports or crutches. One would hope that the people involve in that type of business would essentially dwell in wanting to help others with their challenges and enhance their quality of life, before the incentive of making money.

CHAPTER NINE

What Others Think Should Not Be Our Concern

I became more and more dependent on wearing wigs instead of hair clips or hair pieces because it was less time consuming thus more simple. I had enough trying to handle thin, frizzy hair and at times patches of hair would be found on the pillow upon rising in the morning. I was proud of the fact that I had developed an effective method where I had one wig for every occasion in my life. I had a wig for skiing, another one for my evening outings, and a wig for daily life and so on.

Some of my family members began commenting on my daily head wear. They would sometimes pass negative comments. They did not show support and did not understanding the extent of what I had been through for years. They seemed to think that I was just having some fun wearing different things on my head in the name of vanity or fashion.

One evening, during a hot July summer night, we were having dinner at my sister-in-laws. Around the table were my cousins, my two brothers and their wives and my nephew. The atmosphere so far was joyful and convivial. The atmosphere changed when someone said that she preferred how I looked like with my own hair. It was completely out of context from the topic we were discussing. Maybe she was tipsy from the wine she had. At that moment, all of a sudden I became the center of attention. They all loudly agreed in unison that these wigs I had been wearing were simply not me. Their voices were like faint whispers in a background as I immediately went deep within like a submarine about to be attacked. What exactly did they mean by the word "me"? In my opinion, this reaction was rather interesting since they all considered themselves being spiritual individuals with an allergy to superficiality.

In my point of view, their behavior and comments were indicators that they had fallen into the mass thinking patterns. I did not react to these comments and did not try to defend my position either. I remained composed and proceeded by telling them that I did not define myself by my hair style or any parts of my body for that matter. I continued saying that wigs for me were simply another accessory that I would adjust in the morning the same way I would adjust my pants, my shirt and my shoes. I did not get any reaction from them on that statement. They just changed the topic.

That episode with my family forced me to make sense of it all in order to understand where this discussion came from. We had been raised in a family where education was based on deep values. My father came from a heritage where noble thoughts, speech, and dignified actions prevailed. My dad always lived without judging or complying with superficiality. He was profoundly rooted in this amazing expanded awareness. For him, action always spoke louder than words. He never tried to oppress us with his religious convictions and he certainly never tried to evangelize any of us. I never heard one negative comment coming from his mouth even in situations where it could have been so tempting. No, instead, he always chose constructive and beneficial verbal expressions.

Throughout his life, my father taught us not only deep values but a beautiful high code ethics. His spirituality was lived and demonstrated daily. Needless to say that it is the reason why that type of conversation my family held at the dinner table left me puzzled.

I must highlight the fact that the hair my brothers and sister once loved no longer existed. It was in the past tense. I am grateful that life's circumstances helped me successfully master depression and enabled me to survive and learn from every strange situation one faces with hair loss. I did it on my own. I did not hire any specialists or therapists to handle for me this situation. I was left to my own device. It is difficult for people who have never been exposed to different challenges due to physical changes or anomalies to have an understanding toward these facts.

We women are major targets for harsh criticisms and judgments relating to physical appearance. We are either too thin, too fat, too tall, too short, too small or too large breasted. We are considered too aggressive when expressing our opinions with strength and passion or too passive when silent. God forbid if we are successful. We become the target of various negative remarks. We can take any gossip magazines from the stands of a supermarket and observe how nasty some of the comments are toward these poor actresses. They show horrible pictures of them and zoom on their flaws. It is as if an unhealthy and sick pleasure has developed over the years among the population.

I learned the hard way that criticisms of all types we hear around must not be absorbed inside. We should filter out negativity and only let in constructive words. My filter is shaped with lucid discernment throughout these experiences. If I had a daughter, I would guide her through these tormented seas and high waves by telling her that the spirit living within us is the main driver and the main operator of our body and that same spirit has the power to create and choose which way we want to go.

It is essential to develop a solid point of self-awareness within so we can quickly filter what we see, read and hear and the younger we do that the better it will be for our overall health. These filtering strategies will enable us how to process information we receive every day. It is of the utmost importance to develop a healthy sense of discrimination so that we only keep the data that will promote our growth and evolution. That way, we will avoid an overload on our "hard drive' and will delete all unnecessary and useless information. We always seem to pay attention on our intake of good nutritious foods for our body and why not pay the same attention regarding the kind of food we feed our mind with.

Opinions are just that; "opinions". Opinions are like navels we all have one. What others think should not be our concern in terms of creating our lives. Unless we ask for it on our own volition. We spend way too much of our lives looking for outside validation and approval that eludes us. It turns out it is an inside job. It all happens inside ourselves thus why it is essential to go inward without fear. We have no control on other people's thinking process but we certainly have control on our own thoughts.

It is different when we ask close friends what their thinking is on something in order to help elucidate a problem we are faced with. We listen to what they have to say about it and we are then in a position to make up our own minds, ultimately choosing exactly how we will handle the situation. Otherwise we should not be bothered. We have to constantly remind ourselves that we cannot meet everyone's expectations, demands, tastes or points of views. We cannot change anyone except ourselves. We cannot please everyone's wishes.

CHAPTER TEN

Life's Ups and Downs

Allow me to go back to the time when I had just returned from upstate New York where we had spread my sister's ashes in the nearby forest where she had lived with her husband. A few days later, I thought it would be good for me to go shopping in order to shift my attention somewhere else. As a woman I know shopping can have a magical power. I called my good buddy Lea and off we went shopping until we dropped. As I was sitting in front of a glass case trying various watches, my girlfriend stood behind me looking at handbags. She put a hat on my head as a joke and suddenly she said out loud these words I will never forget: "Oh My God girl, I can see your scalp"...My heart went down to my toes as I could not believe what was happening again. The monster of Alopecia had returned. Under the circumstances I had gone through with the tragedy of my sister's passing, it came as no surprise. Unfortunately, at that point, I was not emotionally equipped to deal with that problem again. I only had enough strength to heal the void from the tragic loss and nothing else. I was barely there myself.

The next morning, after this incidence with Lea, I went into a panic mode and felt overwhelmed by insecurities, self-doubt and despair. What was I to do with the rest of my physical life as a young woman precociously loosing hair? We associate youth of the body with healthy hair, glowing skin and beautiful teeth.

This event clearly showed me how life consists of ups and downs. No situations remain the same. Our well-being depends on so many variables. Sometimes we feel strong and invincible and think we have arrived at the top of our game, our final destination where we can put our defense mechanisms finally down. Little do we know that, from time to time, according to certain given conditions, we can easily slip back to a place of less gains where we will once more be required strength and vigilance? Our lives as we know can drastically change from one moment to the next. It is how we handle this constant change that will make our existence good or bad.

We strive for perfection all our life willingly ignoring the eventual endings to our story. We could win the lottery and radically leave behind us an existence of total destitution and rise into amazing material heights. We could have an accident that would alter our quality of life forever. In both cases, these circumstances contribute to huge shifts and changes. The question is are we equipped with the necessary psychological ammunition to help us face these possibilities with strength.

It seems that life consists of two major movements, one consists of progression and the other deals with regression. One thing is for sure is that life never stays the same. In my opinion, all movements we go through in our existence are worth it because it is the only way we can grow and learn. It is not always fun to be on a roller coaster because the fear of falling is always there but if we approach the roller coaster with a sense of surrender, the ride becomes easier and smoother.

One morning I decided that I would stand in front of my bedroom mirror unclothed with no wig or makeup. I looked straight at my reflection, free of judgment and artifice almost as if it was the first time I was seeing this person in front of me in the mirror. All of a sudden I felt my true identity (my soul) revealing itself with grace and acceptance. In that instant all the nasty incessant little voices of criticism inside my head went silent and only peace remained. It felt as if I had thrown all useless apparels out the window and kept the essence of my being. That experience left me with a profound sensation of relief and freedom.

It amazes me to observe how we have a tendency to set unrealistic expectations for ourselves physically and mentally. The example that comes to mind is the touching story about a girl called Mona. Mona was born pudgy with sturdy short limbs. Since she was a kid, she nurtured the dream to become a prima ballerina. She was completely consumed by that fervent desire. Maybe in another world she could have been that dancer but not in the reality of the world of classical ballet. When one joins a ballet company, it is a known fact that the physical criteria and demands are unforgiving. Her body type did not fit in the main criteria of ballerinas.

What was Mona to do? Give up that dream? Or try to choose a career that could still involve her in the same world of ballet but on a different level such as choreography, scenography or costume design? There was a big discrepancy between her desire and the physical reality in which she had been born. It goes to show you that the sooner we come to terms with the fact that there will always be prettier, uglier, taller, thinner, richer or more destitute people than us, the better it is. We have to realize that we are part of a world filled with "diversity". Diversity makes our world much more interesting. It would be boring if we all looked the same, thought the same and did the same things.

The lessons I have learned during my life might be futile and uninteresting to my neighbors, however, sharing our trials and tribulations with one another can be healthy and vital to our wellbeing as a society. It can only bring positive results. We might feel it would make things much easier by pretending that all was good and happy bypassing chances to be real toward each other by expressing our true feelings. It would enhance kindness and compassion in our hearts. We could remind one another that in fact, we all are constantly work in progress.

We must never give up when we are faced with adversity because the slightest efforts we make will contribute to a healthy growth. Soon or later, all of us independently from our social status are bound to accumulate scars and face rough patches in the quilt of our existence. This is the stuff that makes our life's suitcase light or heavy. Every day we have the choice of being constructive or destructive. This choice comes with consequences. We must stay lucid and frequently reassess our priorities. The questions we must ask ourselves on a regular basis are: do we want to go deeper in the physical superficiality of life or go deeper into spiritual awareness? Do we want to come from a place of EGO or a place of authenticity? Do we want to be part of the wild rat race? Do we want to come from a place of fear or a place of love? Are our goals set up toward more accumulation of material possessions or develop more understanding of our true purpose. If we choose the latter, our understanding of life will widen and expand exponentially. We will eliminate complicated melodramas thus live with simplicity. By simplicity I do not mean destitution and deprivation but rather a genuine approach toward all given conditions.

It is essential to develop inner stability in order to avoid being affected by change. This is the foundation for each and every one of us since we all are in it together. Whether we are poor, rich, disabled, sick or at the top of our game, we all go through difficult times in our lives. From the outside, we may look physically different and we may live different realities but behind the body resides the master of ceremony. That master is the silent witness to our trials and tribulations and can take other directions and make various choices depending on where one wants to go and what one wants to achieve.

We live in a time where sharing information through social networks can be either destructive to oneself or constructive and informative. We, as human beings all strive for one essential element; it is happiness and no matter what language we speak, what culture we grew up in or what faith we have, the quest for happiness is indeed a universal language which transcends all relative variations.

CHAPTER ELEVEN

My Dinner with Helga

I met my friend Helga a few years ago on a beautiful hot summer day. She was sitting alone by the South side of the community pool, reading a book. My husband and I introduced ourselves to her. She was a beautiful, dark haired woman, probably in her early sixties. She looked like Sofia Loren. As we exchanged a few words with her, we detected a German accent. Promptly, my husband exchanged a few words with her in German. She was taken by surprise and as it so happened, they both discovered they were from the same region in Germany, near Hamburg. The three of us immediately felt great affinity. We became friends from that moment on.

Every sunny day, around three o'clock, Helga would walk to the pool and sit at the same spot on the same chair with a book. Sometimes she would shy away from us and some other times she would engage in an intense discussion about her life, her childhood memories from her country. She definitely had many interesting stories to tell.

She had been raised in the early fifties with strict discipline. In those days, the gap between boys and girls was big. Rules were tight. Girls' voices and opinions mattered less than those of boys. What prevailed during that era was that women were taught how to become perfect queens of the household. It subsequently created a disempowered future for many women of that generation. Most of these women were confined to tasks such as raising kids, cooking and cleaning. The tendency to be submissive prevailed. However, let us not generalize since it is within that same generation that our society witnessed the rise of very powerful women, famous writers, activists, political figures who were not afraid to fight for their rights. These women stood at the forefront of feminist movements.

When Helga married her husband Reinhardt, they both decided to open up a lucrative business in their German town. They immediately engendered amazing financial success and were living a good and prosperous life. She had two lovely sons. In the early eighties, they took a major decision to leave their country to settle in the United States. The reason behind that move was to make the American dream their own. They opted for a warm place. They lived a good life in Florida and the kids went to school there. They created a lovely and nurturing home for their children. Life was good, very good actually. Then, one day at the snap of a finger that perfect life dramatically changed forever. Her youngest son was discovered lifeless in his bed before school. He had overdosed on prescription drugs.

She revealed to me that the discovery of her son lying there, motionless and lifeless was like someone had cut her four limbs all at once. As the years went by she never forgot the pain and somehow just barely managed to live with it. Sadness grew deeper in her heart and soul. She never quite recovered from that loss. Her husband fell into a severe and massive depression as it generally is a frequent reaction. My own parents lost two children and my mother told me: "losing your child is the worst thing that can happen to a parent, one never forgets the pain of that loss but learns to live with that pain"

I gradually discovered more about Helga's life every time we got together. One evening I invited her at my house for dinner. It was during the Christmas holidays, and I thought it would do us good to cook together, have some wine and chill out. My husband was absent that evening. It was a perfect atmosphere to have some good woman to woman downtime. We cooked a succulent meal, laughed a lot during the preparation of our elaborated fancy menu. The atmosphere was relaxed and we felt very close to each other. We shared ideas, recipes, feelings and experiences. At around nine o'clock, while sitting in front a crackling fireplace, sitting at the table lit with candles, I sensed Helga becoming more somber in her speech. I detected vulnerability in the tone of her voice. I saw tears welling down her cheeks as she proceeded in telling me a secret. She shared the truth about the circumstances surrounding her son's death. She cried even more when she said how devastating that terrible loss had been on her health and her body.

She further added that the tragedy had caused her much distress on many levels. Among them was an increase in serious hair loss over the years. Wearing a full wig for her had never been an option until her situation became very hard to handle. All of a sudden she let out a deep sigh and went silent as if I had pressed the mute button on the TV. She was lost in her thoughts and her eyes filled with tears and profound sadness. She sat there quietly staring at the candles with sorrow. All of a sudden, she raised her right arm and with great courage pulled her wig off to show me the devastation that had occurred and what was left of her hair. Needless to say that I was completely submerged with disbelief. After a few seconds, on my own volition, I followed her strength and did the same. We looked at each other as if we were both totally naked and bared our souls in total surrender, like two soldiers who surrender to the enemy by putting their weapons down. The enemy in this case being hair loss.

This moment of truth was such an empowering moment for both of us. It was a beautiful communion, filled with highly charged emotions between two women, two friends. That special moment allowed us to reveal ourselves in our authenticity with no fear of rejection. We had nothing to hide, no pretense but just the real "us". I knew we were two women among thousands and thousands all over the world suffering in secret with the same ailment.

Her husband died not long after that night. Under the circumstances, a few months following his death, she judged that it would be better for her mental and physical health if she moved back to Florida.

A year or so after the death of her partner, she felt it was time for her to consider meeting other men. She started going out with other single widowed women in order to eventually meet someone. She confided in me that she was petrified at the thought of meeting a new man. Just the thought of intimacy with that person gave her such anxiety. She had been with the same man, her husband for over thirty years. What would she tell the new partner about her condition, i.e., wigs? She knew that, soon or later, the fatal moment of truth would inexorably come. She felt handicapped. How does someone approach such awkward situations when the crucial moment of intimacy is near? All these questions and vulnerability run deep in the skin of anyone facing these types of issues. It is obvious that these delicate situations are not only with intimacy but can also easily be found in other scenarios.

Here is one good example of such awkward moments from my personal experience. During a trip to an exotic tropical island with my husband, we stayed with one of his good business partners, Matthew. He and his wife are serious scuba divers, and snorkelers. One day, Matthew suggested we all go on his boat and go in the deep end of the bay to snorkel at large where the most beautiful corals in the region were. That coral was far from the shore. We could see the most beautiful species of fish there. There we were, in the depths of the West Indian Ocean. This was going to be an exhilarating experience for everyone. However, from my point of view, just thinking about the prospect of deep diving represented a serious trouble for me. From the moment I found out we were going snorkeling in the deep sea, a signal of "red alert" a potential nightmare was waiting at the corner. I felt threatened in my world.

At first, my immediate reaction was to find a good excuse not to go along with them however, very quickly decided to not give power to this obstacle. I just had to figure out which wig would work best in that situation. I had to consider how tight it would have to be, how I would make it look natural while going underwater. During that assessment, I felt sadness and frustration. What a waste of life I thought. There was nothing in the world I would have loved more than to just put my hair up in a ponytail and walk out freely with the wind blowing on my face without a care in the world. It was not so. It was complicated. I did survive and somehow managed to avoid a disaster and humiliation, should I had lost the prosthesis while diving. I thank God nothing happened that day. My caring husband constantly checked on me during the entire boat trip. It was endearing and I felt grateful to have him in my life.

So many people, so many different lives, so many scenarios and destinies, some lighter than others and some filled with one challenge after another. From one minute to the next, what we think is a certainty can very well disappear at the snap of a finger. How can we approach such variables? It is as if we are constantly walking on a wire and each movement counts in determining what the next moment will be like. There is an impact for each step we take. When we claim we are in total control of our lives, I rise my eyebrows a bit. We have control over the choices we make such as the food we eat, how much physical exercise we do, our work ethics, the kind of friends we hang out with, the words we speak, the thoughts we feed our minds and the types of movies or TV programs we watch. We certainly have control over the attitude we have toward circumstances.

We are the driving force with these individual choices but when we are dealing with the complexities of the world we live in these days, it is another game. Our society is filled with numerous belief systems and different religions in various parts of the planet. This reality simply surpasses our personal volitions. How can we control people who live in countries on the other extremity of the planet who have realities that are diametrically opposite to ours? There is a huge gap between the reality of someone who lives in the heart of downtown New-York and someone who lives in Central Africa for instance or Indonesia. The value systems cannot be the same for each continent. Cultures are based on climate, geography, and language and religion background. It would be unfair to try to homogenize all these to one autocratic system. So many civilizations tried that and history shows it never succeeded. The only success that resulted from these conquests were much blood and lost lives.

We have control on how we approach experiences whether they are positive or negative. Will we see the glass half full or half empty or just simply be grateful that we have a glass. Will we make the best out of each given moment or cave in defeat by feeling like a victim. This is where we have the power and it is up to us.

We can always wonder why things are the way they are with our given lives. Why something happens to this person and not that one. Why one has it easy and the other carries a heavy load all their life. Why in some car accident one person will die and the other will survive? Why is one born in the same family from the same parents, given the same DNA and genetic inheritance and yet look so different from the other siblings?

One of my siblings was born premature. He had physical deformities. He always has been physically and mentally challenged. What puzzles me is that he had been given the same genetic heritage from my father and mother. Yet he was so different from the rest of us. Having been raised in a Catholic family, the answer as to the reason why remained a grey zone. The ultimate explanation from a Catholic point of view would be that his suffering was not in vain because it would help him gain a good place in heaven. That answer never satisfied my hungry inquisitive mind.

One great saint from the Far East once said simply, "The laws of Karma are unfathomable" (ref. 3). Every religion has a common denominator with that universal justice of 'what goes around comes around'. The only difference is it is expressed differently. If we do not give these universal laws importance then we will always have the same question "Why" why me, why her, why them? With no answer ever. I have always been a sincere seeker so I dared searching in a proactive way for available information and this, among millions of printed materials in the fields of philosophy and spirituality.

In my quest for answers, I had a preference for Eastern philosophies. I also got involved in comparative studies of all religions of the world. I noticed that each of them had their foundation based on similar paradigms, metaphors and archetypes. What prevails in the chore structures of all philosophies is the evidence of a universal justice. Obviously the existence of that element does not necessarily alleviate the pain and torments that come along with physical or mental challenges. The main thing is allow human beings to live their lives in dignity and courage. I know it has always been a sad struggle to this day for my sibling in spite of all the love we constantly showed him. I have grown to love him the way he is, since for me love is the most essential and vital element for healthy survival.

At the end of the day it does not matter what we believe in or which religion we belong to as long as we commit to it with sincerity and integrity. My sibling is who he is, with what life gave him in this time and space. It seems he has learned quite well how to handle his present condition. More power to him!

CHAPTER TWELVE

Life Is Like A Movie

When we enter an empty theater and the movie is not yet there, what we see is a large white silver screen. Once the movie projection starts, we become so absorbed in the story that we completely forget there is a screen until the movie ends. What happened to the screen? It was indeed always there. Same with our spirit and true self, it is always there but somehow it gets overshadowed by all the pictures in our heads, in our lives, all the melodramas we constantly create with which we get so attached to. We lose awareness of the underlying "I". Somewhere in time these pictures we project daily take precedence. We start believing in our own story and our scenarios thinking this is as good and as real as it gets.

We become identified with our projections. This reminds me of an interesting analogy. Let's say we are on a beach and standing there in the sand with the sun on our back. Looking down we clearly see the reflection of our body. We know that reflection is not us. We could do the same with our spirit living in the body. I like to think that we are like actors on a stage and we get to pick a role we want to play and choose the costume that will fit the role. The danger lays in forgetting who we were before the play started. It is similar with when we choose a career in life and do it for so many years. We become that career so much so that when it is time to retire, we do not want to give up the idea that we had defined ourselves by that career. Many people get depressed when they retire mostly because of a limited identification with whatever they were.

Hair or no hair? Perfect skin or flawed skin... Fat versus

skinny....? Tall versus short? Witty versus dumb? All these traits do not define us in a complete manner. They are temporary elements which can change at any given time and space according to various conditions. Except of course the height of one's body.

I have a friend of mine, whom I shall call Magen. In my opinion Magen is one the most beautiful souls I have ever encountered. Her beauty and candid innocence are larger than life. Yet, she has no clue how powerful and beautiful she is. Why? Because somewhere on the time line of her life, she got caught in the drama of her childhood memories. Depression sank in and she had to take antidepressants. Over the years she became obese. She disconnected from her inner beauty which the first thing everyone sees when they meet her.

The beauty of living in a collectivity is that everyone has a story to tell. We all have amazing things to share and sad things too. We are unique in every aspect of our being, unique from the inside out. No one is identical. This uniqueness creates the book of human life. All interconnected complexities which contribute in the creation of our forever changing human history, decades after decades, and centuries after centuries. The amazement of multiple unique realities coexisting and sharing time and space simultaneously on the same planet.

Women have a tendency to criticize, scrutinize, and judge themselves and others harshly. I recall one summer night on a full moon in July having fun with five girlfriends. We decided to go skinny dipping in a nearby pool. When we arrived, my first reaction was to run to the little shack to turn the lights switches on so the pool would be all lit up and create magic. It created waves of blue and turquoise reflecting on the surface of the water like a fairy tale. Alas, most women voted against these lights claiming it would show too much of their bodily imperfections. I felt disappointed since we were just having fun like when we were kids and we would jump in the pool with innocence and spontaneity swimming with the flow without any restrain or hindrance. Body issues took precedence in that moment and overruled the experience. These issues sometimes rule our entire existence more often than not and at the end of the day depletes our enthusiasm and joy. This is an obvious rubbery in the name of a wild quest for physical perfection.

We need to shift our obsession to another level. Many approaches such as meditation, yoga, stretching the limbs and deep breathing (pranayama) and creative visualization can help do that. We have so many options and alternatives these days and we must follow our inner voice as to what will work best for us.

We have to be aware that the word "yoga" these days is often misused for trendy and fashion reasons. What does the word yoga really mean? Many books were written on the subject throughout the ages. One common definition we find in many of these books is that yoga means union with self the practice of yoga enables perfect fusion of body and mind. It is quite shocking to observe that so many places in North America offer yoga classes as a mean to build muscle mass or flatten the belly. One can only laugh because it reflects once again how madly body obsessed and narcissistic our society can be.

Five thousand years ago, Patanjali elaborated one of the most detailed systems based on the eight limbs (aspects) of yoga. These limbs work systematically in symphony with one another and are part of an entire solid foundation. The purpose is to develop higher states of awareness. In that spirit, yoga becomes an integral and transformative practice to permanently change one's perceptions.

These old techniques have existed for one purpose: to bring the individual to a level of awareness where the soul (atman) is unaffected by the pictures projected in the mind. Behind the curtain of images, the soul remains untouched, unshaken. Beyond this mental commotion of the monkey race of thoughts exists a place of utter infinite silence. That silence transcends the incessant activities of wanting, desiring and craving insatiably for more. That is when we start a serious healing of emotional and mental scars.

Narcissism prevails in a society which thrives on success, power, social status and wealth. It is exacerbated in big cities where people tend to create their reality based on external values. Our world is filled with "ism" in the structures of our words from fanatic to criticism and paroxysm.

In some parts of the world we live in decadent material abundance while in other parts we find severe constriction, restriction, oppression and poverty. It is fascinating to observe how belief systems create opposition and rivalry, resulting inevitably in gruesome wars. It comes from fear, the fear of losing power and control.

It does not matter which beliefs we comply to nor does it matter what religion we embrace as long as its results in making us better people and bring more positivity in our immediate environment and into the world. There are only few places on the planet which operate in total harmony despite individual differences and hierarchy. They function on the basic foundation that each person has a unique useful role to play in the bigger picture which contributes in the creation of a healthy place to live in. Each role is considered as equal and important as the other. Each person is treated with dignity and respect. Statistics demonstrate that such quality of life eliminates criminal tendencies. Negative emotions such as anger, hate, jealousy and competitive aggressive behaviors are not predominant. Bhutan is a country worth studying in its social structures for that matter. They apply the rules of happiness for all in every layer of their community. Happiness is their essential national growth product.

CHAPTER THIRTEEN

Healed by a Great Saint

It was during a cold October evening when my husband received a call from a director of an international organization located in Holland. At that time, my husband's business had been very successful promoting Canadian high tech companies for projects in the Pacific Rim. Holland was the head office of this international organization and they wanted to meet with him to discuss a large scale development project. The next day we were on a plane to Amsterdam. We arrived at the headquarters and after a long and nerve wrecking wait we finally got to meet this great spiritual teacher. He had heard about my husband's undertakings in many countries all around the world. We walked into a large meeting room where business men, bankers, magicians, artists, designers from all over the world were sitting. Needless to say that I was impressed by the presence of such high profile individuals sitting all together in the same hall.

When we walked into that room, we immediately were taken by a sense of relief and peace. I thought this could be like heaven. There were many beautiful flowers surrounding his seat. Sweet fragrances and aromas exuding from the hyacinths and roses of all kinds. Flower smells were mixed with incense which made the atmosphere almost outer worldly, beyond earthly perceptions. There he was, this amazing Master in his white robe sitting in a perfect lotus position on a sofa totally still and smiling. I experienced a sense of familiarity and immediately felt as if I was coming home. I felt safe like being wrapped in a soft beautiful cashmere blanket. It was as if I had entered into this cosmic womb or dome where nothing bad could no longer reach me. A vortex of celestial light. In a charming melodious Indian accent he ordered us to join him with the rest of the crowd.

His Presence was imposing and reverberated in every fiber of our body. My husband and I both simultaneously felt an amazing immediate shift of physical transformation. It is a challenging task trying to translate in words and try to give justice to the experience of being in the presence of a great sage. That meeting was something I had never gone through on this earth. I have been to the Great Pyramids, to the Great Wall of China, to the Eiffel Tower, to Versailles and the Vatican however, nothing absolutely nothing of that magnitude came close to that when we met him the first time.

Because of my limited ability to convey this other worldly experience with exactitude I inserted this brilliant explanation written by a well-known doctor which also joins theories in Quantum Physics. " Quantum physics suggest the universe is made up of vibrational waves which influence masses of physical objects by an interaction of different frequencies. Light, motion, sound and time are all inter-related in physical space. Thus if the vibrational waves operate from higher frequencies we automatically feel it and react to it by changing our own vibrational wave with it."

He concluded that both our spiritual and physical consciousness project and receive light energy.(.....) as souls, the density, color, and form of light we radiate is proportional to the power of our knowledge and perception as represented by increasing concentrations of light matter as we develop. Individual patterns of energy not only display who we are, but indicate the degree of ability to heal others. (Ref.4)

This beautiful elaboration from Dr. Newton could explain why when people met this Sage they unanimously felt a direct and drastic palpable change in their frequencies and vibrational fields of energy.

Upon our entrance, the sage looked at me right in the eyes as if he was reading and scanning my soul right through. With a sweet tone of voice he said that it was good that I had come after all.

I will tell you why these words hit me as a lightning. Before leaving home to hop on a plane and join my husband on the trip to Holland, I had been hesitant because the invitation had not been extended to me personally. I went with my inner feeling and as the story will later demonstrate it was indeed the right choice. It pays off after all when we listen to that little voice inside.

It is important to mention that at that time in my life I was going through tormented emotional rough seas inside. Let's just say that there was more darkness than light permeating in my thinking processes within. The dichotomy was that I was fully aware I had been given many beautiful talents and yet had not managed to bring them to fruition for whatever reasons. When we have goals and do not seem to achieve them, the result ends up in frustration.

One day, the saint sent my husband to a far distant African country. I asked him if I could go him and without hesitation he replied that it would not be such a good idea since I would come back so tired. He strongly recommended that I stay put. It is important for me to mention that the lineage where this saint came from was deeply rooted in the old Vedic traditions of the Vedas. This knowledge has a multitude of sacred texts which are solely passed by oral recitations and this, from one generation to another generation leaving out possible wrong interpretations and translations of these texts. Therefore in this oral communication of wisdom purity of the knowledge is kept intact. He came from a direct lineage of the Shankar Acharya of the North. He was a simple monk with no worldly possessions except a Dhoti (Indian word for robe), and sandals. Very similar to Gandhi. Women were allowed to be in his presence only by formal official invitation.

We could compare this protocol with the Catholic nuns and priests who live in cloisters. They are allowed visits through special requests. I have accompanied my mother many times to visit one of her aunts who lived in a cloister. This was quite an interesting experience that created deep impressions in my memory. The smell of church incense and voices heard from a far distance at the end of long empty corridors, echoing crystal clear high tone voices from nuns who would chant Gregorian texts. It was haunting and yet so beautiful. I felt it was like a choir of angels singing from heaven. As a kid I had a fertile imagination.

Alright let us go back to Holland now. It was a few days after my husband had left that I found myself alone in a hotel room. I was experiencing a deep emotional pain again in the dark abyss of my soul and was sobbing. I could not pinpoint where this profound sadness was coming from. I felt isolated and disconnected from the rest of the world. You could compare the experience with when you travel in foreign countries and you don't speak the language. I basically felt like an outsider basically all my life, on and off. A sense of not belonging to any place really. Not being able to relate to anything or anyone. It was such an uncomfortable state of being. I no longer wanted that pain and decided I had enough. I decided that night that I would cease my physical life. In my view, there was only one way out of this trap.

Since my hotel was very close to the home of the great sage, I felt I owed it to myself to at least try to meet with him one way or another. I called his first secretary and asked for an audience knowing that my chances were slim. The secretary reacted with kindness and put me on hold. That moment felt like eternity. While on hold, I sat on a chair in a fetus position staring at his photograph. I prayed with such fervor and begged the universe with sincerity and intensity to grant me this last wish. In the secret of my heart, I was telling the sage why I wanted to meet with him. I knew he was the only being on earth at that strategic and precarious moment, who had the power to heal me and save me from tragedy.

The secretary came back on the phone and said it was perfectly fine for me to come and meet with him. I felt so elated that I just put on a dress over my yoga pants and hastily walked out of the hotel. As I exited the hotel, I deeply knew that my life was inevitably about to be transformed forever. It was about to be the most life altering moment ever.

When I arrived in his private suite, there was a meeting that was just about to end. Twenty people were present. I quietly took a seat in the back row, trying to be invisible. The sage did not look at me or acknowledge my presence and it was fine with me because I felt honored to be silently witnessing a meeting in his presence. I felt grateful to be there with one of the greatest sages this planet has ever seen. There had been a famously known Rock band which had studied with him in India many years ago. They spent months in his presence in order to learn about his wise spiritual insights, visions and deep vast wisdom. I had to pinch myself to make sure this was not a dream. There I was, a broken little girl carrying inside me the heavy weight of sorrows, flirting with suicide. The challenges of Alopecia had taken their tale on my soul taking away my joy for life. I felt nurtured in that room as if we were surrounded by a shield of invincibility. Sitting there with luminaries from the four corners of the world was a true privilege. The healing began during that night.

Was it a coincidence or was it by the grace of God that these events and circumstances aligned themselves to bring me there to avoid an action that would have been devastating? I am now convinced without a doubt that there is a plan, a cosmic one where all things align themselves in their proper place at the right moment without any involvement of one's own volition. I did not decide nor chose to be in this turn of events. Obviously something greater than me did orchestrate this plan. It is not as if I woke up one morning and said:" Gee I am going to book a flight to Holland because I want to meet that great saint everyone has been talking about. It was something much bigger and more powerful than personal will.

To support this concept of perfect synchronicity of events, here is an excerpt from one of my favorite authors, Barbara Marciniak. She wrote once: "When, against all odds, a series of personally meaningful events unfold in a timely, yet unusual manner to shed light and profound insight on a situation, you are getting a glance into the infinite splendor of the multilayered world of significance. In the field of existence, time has no bounds; events are connected and enriched with the purposeful weavings of all forms of consciousness learning how to play the field." (ref.5)

From that moment, I surrendered to the great cosmic field of all possibilities. The meetings which would take place in the private clusters of this sacred room were constantly filled with great writers, scientists, music composers. It was mind boggling and fascinating. Needless to say it was inspiring, uplifting and very informative on all levels. Day after day I felt all horizons surrounding me were stretching to infinity.

The saint incessantly met some of the greatest creative minds of the world. Businessmen, country leaders, world renowned artists, as well as inventors. His creative genius was such that he would engage with amazing ease in whatever field of knowledge his guests were involved in. It was as if all his life he had thoroughly studied all these topics and was an expert in all of them. From science to international politics to economics to environmental issues. He would navigate with such facility, passion, tremendous interest and joy. What also struck me while we were in his presence was the fact that he could sit in these meetings which would frequently linger for over 14 -15 hours. He would not once get up or take a break or excuse himself. In the meantime, many of us would have to excuse ourselves for a few minutes either to drink water or go to the loo.

Every person who met with him shared a similar deep sense of reverence toward him. No matter how important the person was, whether it was the president of some African country or the owner of the largest international company, or respected dignitaries, they would feel a genuine admiration toward him while in his presence. He had an amazing ability to go so deep in every single minute detail of any given field. If one was working on a project of architecture or publishing a book, he would always bring in the most insightful angles that no one had considered before. His thinking was indeed larger than life.

He always thought outside the box. He broke all set boundaries and challenged all existing paradigms and old beliefs in a creative, constructive manner. It was in one's own best interest to leave all preconceived ideas and limited ways of thinking behind the door prior to meeting him.

To this day I feel extremely grateful that life spared me from committing suicide. All I can say is that when someone is in deep despair and fervently addresses his/her inner demons to a greater power, it will no doubt bring its timely unfolding results in its due time.

Let me go back to that first meeting I had with him. When the meeting adjourned, the great saint commented on how good the evening went. Everyone proceeded to leave the room and so did I. He looked in my direction and said with a sweet tone of voice: "no, no not you, please sit and wait". I looked behind me to see who he was talking to when I realized I was alone, totally alone with him. He looked at me with such kindness and sweet candor and asked if I knew where my husband was and if I had a phone number where to call him. I replied that I did. So we called my husband at his hotel and spoke to him. It was such a loving exchange filled with kindness. Once the telephone conversation ended, he looked at me and said gently in a soft tone of voice that it was good and we should meet like that every night...

He took me in a subtle way under his wing. He never once asked me anything about my mental state or inner reality....I knew that He knew. His clairvoyance and sharp insights unraveled in the most profound way so that the healing process could occur. His strategy was simple, effective and mostly filled with love and compassion. He was the embodiment of gentleness and kindness. He took me step by step into recovery with grace, compassion and care, just as a kind father would do with his beloved daughter. I felt I was in the presence of my Cosmic Father.

He knew right away I needed a purpose, a focus and a

healthy meaningful direction. This had to be independent from the relationship I had with my husband. It is probably why he made me stay in Holland on my own.

The lessons I got from listening to the meetings that I attended were very important. One of the lessons is that we often make choices based upon our likes or dislikes, attractions or aversions when in fact, ideally our decisions should come from a deep level of our existence, that would be independent of these factors above. It is said in many philosophies that the true purpose of our human life is to ultimately reach total fulfillment on all levels of our being. The question is how can we achieve and access such a level? Many specialists in the field of psychology, spirituality and philosophy have their own take on these fundamental issues. Each take has its own color, flavor and angle and at the end of the day, it is going to be your decision to see what resonates best with you.

When I met this great master, my truth revealed itself in such an effortless, beautiful way that it deleted all bad and misconceived past memories, as if my inner sky had always been cloudy and all of a sudden cleared up to let the sun shine through .It was amazing because all the thoughts that rose in my mind were good, kind and loving toward myself. The self-criticism, self-condemnation and self-hatred stopped all at once. The monkey mind had finally shut up. For the first time since the day I was born, I was free of all negativity inherited from my mother and family members and felt a sense of lightness in the heart and a big relief. I could actually see a true and authentic beauty in front of me, inside and outside. It was my moment of "Grace". The "Ah ha" moment people describe.

Human nature being human, I confess to you that from time to time I do experience old negative tendencies of self-deprecation and harshness but the difference is they are no longer controlling my inner peace and happiness. They are like passerby. There is a certain detachment toward all these types of thoughts and emotions.

The challenge we all face in this fast paced world of appearances is how to maintain our spiritual integrity throughout our day to day life. Every day we are confronted with various scenarios, situations that could either go in the best direction possible or in the most undesirable place. How can we succeed in developing equanimity while experiencing either easiness, difficulty or adversity? The constant rat race we live in can easily decimate a person's self-worth thus why we must be well prepared and equipped on all levels of our life.

The legacy this sage will have left behind is vast in its impact on society and infinite in its influence on us. He truly was a great visionary who foresaw future technological breakthroughs and radical changes on all levels. His highly achieved wisdom and awareness leaves us with practical solutions on how to alleviate mediocrity, suffering and misery. He taught us that it is possible to stop focusing and analyzing the darkness by simply bring in the light that is needed everywhere, like turning on a switch in a dark room and light appears. Each of us need to readjust, shift and change our agreed accepted old paradigms into a creative new perspective so our horizons and hopes shine bright and now more than ever.

CHAPTER FOURTEEN

It Goes to Show You

The other day, I went to my favorite store for wigs and accessories. I had not been there for months. I know all the sales ladies there. They have become my extended family throughout the years. Most of them come from West Africa. When I go there I feel I am in their country. They are always greeting me with such joy and genuine hugs. However, when the time came for me to try a wig, to my great surprise I realized they did not have a private room anymore for those of us who are bald and do not want to display our handicap to the rest of the world to see. I asked why they didn't provide a place anymore and she replied that there was no more place for that. I explained to her that if one bought wigs just for the fun of it then that is fine but for those who have endured ailments and hair loss that would be a very uncomfortable situation.

The place was packed with black people and there was no corner, not even a dressing room anywhere to privately try a wig. At one point, I noticed that most people who were there were just buying these things for fun and I was probably the only one there at that moment feeling uncomfortable. It made me think of all the people who are truly handicapped in wheel chairs and how they must feel when they go somewhere which does not provide appropriate devices to make their lives easier under their given conditions. It goes to show you how much progress we still have to make in our collective awareness. We have to realize sooner than later that the society is filled with individuals who are less fortunate than others and we must extend our compassion and care for their situation.

We as a group must come to terms with our physical differences, from skin color to body sizes, ugly versus pretty. We are over 6 billion people living on this earth and we are bound to meet with an infinite array of variables in our human race. It is called the infinite field of possibilities of our human DNA codes.

Many people I have talked to over the years, while I was a French teacher, soon or later would confide to me about their family background. They all shared one important common denominator in their respective story. These people, my students were accomplished executives with PhDs and Masters Degrees and yet, they were all still carrying within them deep emotional scars. Their stories frequently related to how they were treated unkindly by others or how they felt within their family, families that did not show love, affection. One woman told me that all she heard throughout her adolescence was how ugly and fat she was and that made her fall in self-deprecation. In other testimonies, their wounds were related to mental or psychological differences with other siblings.

I concluded that sadly enough many people have never healed their scars. These people who have kids and have contacts with their colleagues at work, bring along with them these unresolved emotional issues in the workforce. Interestingly enough this is the thread which links us all together and structures the core of our society. A society that operates more often than not under the influence of aberrations and dysfunctional attitudes. All of us co-exist side by side day after day, sharing our spaces and territories with our neighbors and co-workers. The problem is that these unhealed parts of ourselves can create further behavioral dysfunctions. I guess it would explain why sometimes conflicts at work or at home rise. These patterns will extend themselves throughout life in all the given scenarios possible. Would it not be nice to go through the same daily events with compassion and cooperation instead of animosity, aberrations and pettiness or envy?

How can we build a healthy community if we carry around with us all that accumulated emotional baggage? Most of us try hard in coping with the high demands, pressure and stress that come with our modern life. It can be especially challenging in the workplace. Competition, insecurities, dysfunctional behavior, negative and suppressive attitudes rise when one feels threatened by others who appear to be more successful. It can bring envy, jealousy, resentment and invalidation.

It is very common with us humans that when we are exposed to new ideas or new concepts, we feel threatened. The threat comes from the fact that these new elements challenge our old points of references or points of views. It frequently ignites fear in our hearts because change can sometimes be scary. That is especially true with religions. Throughout the centuries, history has witnessed over and over the worst gruesome massacres and loss of lives in the name of beliefs and in the name of God. This attitude breathes self-righteousness, spiritual pride and condescendence. It is unlikely to bring constructive outcomes. As one historian said once "Men never seem to learn throughout recorded history". "History repeats itself only the décor changes".

It would obviously help to come from love and compassion instead of threat and fear. In many cases when philosophers or scientists propose new elements or breakthrough discoveries, oftentimes the common reaction can be one of automatic rejection or ignore and discard these new concepts.

Have you noticed that people who are attached to their own dramas and misery have a tendency to reject constructive solutions that could easily help them? They will find excuses or put a big intellectual wall toward anything that could help them get out of their misery.

When we operate just by instinct and impulse, oftentimes, chaos and entropy predominates. When it is so, accidents of all kinds are more prone to happen.

CHAPTER FIFTEEN

If Only We Could

If only we could reach out to one another without restrain or shyness. It would grow toward a better and happier place. I was in a doctor's office one morning sitting in the waiting room. I was bored and restless. I was a patient with no patience. I could not read so I let myself wondering around observing the crowd in the waiting room. I noticed these people sitting there seemed lost in their own inner world of thinking. We were more or less about 60 people there and yet not one body resembled another, not one similar face. They were all sizes, colors, shapes. My attention zoomed in on a lady who seemed completely absorbed in her book. I noticed that despite the fact her head was tilted down while reading, her hair had stayed in the same angle, motionless. I guess she felt my stare because all of a sudden she looked right at me looking at her. She knew that I knew her secret. One will always recognize another one. She was wearing a wig. It was a beautiful one, beautiful color and shape. She was a very attractive woman in her mid-forties. How did I know? Certainly not because she was an eye sore in the crowd.

I felt a slight embarrassment from her as she blushed. I gently smiled at her with compassion. Walking toward the doctor's office, I was reflecting on how many of us actually feel what she was feeling at that moment. I wanted to take that woman in my arms and share that beautiful quote with her which says that "we ourselves possess beauty when we are true to our own being. Ugliness is in going over to another order. When we are totally ourselves, we are beautiful. In self-ignorance, we are not."

If we women could give each other the grandness of being and embrace who we are and how we are. If we only could one day at a time slowly stop identifying our worth with the body and stop defining ourselves with our looks. It would be a wonderful experience of relief and ease.

Somewhere in our modern life (whatever how we define the word "modern"), we lost perspective of our real nature. All advertisement, all information we see, hear and read, overload our five senses. The result is a massive manipulation of our conscious and unconscious minds. We then start believing that we are our bodies after all and the way we look must therefore be important. We allow ourselves to be brainwashed by thinking we are nobody unless we have in our possession the suggested gadgets, cars, objects with big names and brands that are daily shoved in our brains. Interestingly enough it seems we are in agreement with that strategy in spite of how miserable that makes us experience life. Our new mantra is "it's never good enough, big enough, or not enough period."

During a breast cancer awareness last fall, there was a program on TV. They interviewed four women who had gone through the big "C". One woman had survived breast cancer and had undergone a double mastectomy. These personal revelations from these women touched me deeply because I felt their pain with regard to their loss. Loss of breasts along with the loss of hair, a typical consequence of chemotherapy. Hair and breasts are two major physical components which define one's femininity.

I could somehow relate to the testimonies. I always had very small breasts and this was combined with alopecia. It was a double hit for me, which meant flat chest and hardly any hair. Because of that I learned to develop other strengths in order to define my own femininity on a different level. I had to go inward and in a deep place in my psyche. I realized for my own healthy growth that my feminine identity could not solely exist with the size of my breasts or the thickness of my hair.

During the TV interview, one woman repeatedly said with strong conviction that when she lost her breasts and her hair, she felt she had lost her entire womanhood. Her facial expressions and her body language revealed defeat in the face of adversity. Her challenges were immense and she might never recover from this. It takes such courage and strength in rough seas to solidly hold on to the infinite power of our ocean rather than holding on to the rippling waves on the surface of the ocean.

When we identify ourselves by the size of our breasts or the thickness of our hair we bypass the essence of who we are. These physical traits are an infinitesimal partial expression of ourselves in the totality of our human life. We all are bound soon or later to fall prey of the waves and forget about the mighty ocean. It is tempting to comply with mass collective madness which promotes that the larger the breasts the more attractive we become. Let us not sell our diamond for the price of spinach by saying "the bigger the better". The incessant quest for the bigger house, the bigger car, the bigger job, the better social status can drain our spirit. We are delusional in thinking that by pursuing these dreams we will succeed in securing our happiness and this will guarantee our final "Shangri-La". This approach is highly and obviously questionable.

Men are also becoming more susceptible to fall into the beauty trap. One of my favorite TV journalists once interviewed a popular rock singer from a famous rock band. The singer was wearing a cap like many guys do these days to display their favorite sport teams or cities or favorite cars.

At first, nothing stood out of the ordinary with his looks until the journalist purposefully asked him to remove his cap. The journalist knew the end results. The guest shyly complied with a bit of hesitance. The audience was shocked because he was bald!! They all started cracking jokes as if he could not hear them. He was nervously laughing with them but I could feel his embarrassment let alone his public humiliation in front of millions of viewers. He was a healthy young twenty five years old man and was suffering from Alopecia.

I did not like what I witnessed on public TV that night. People were ridiculing the poor guy because of a physical condition he had not chosen. Instead of bringing the public's attention to his amazing musical talents, they were focusing on his baldness. It is one thing to be ridiculed and humiliated in private but in front of a whole public? They all thought this was really funny. Little compassion was demonstrated there. It seems that human nature can be so cruel and can sink so low with one another.

It comes as no surprise why bullying at school is on the rise these days. There is a vicious need from so many kids to engage in heavy suppression, invalidate those who show obvious differences and sadistically belittling them in public. I went through being bullied myself at school and suicidal thoughts resulted from that. I was twelve years of age. It is a form of violence. Violence takes many shapes and many aspects.

Violence done on women is a contributing factor in generating more misery and suffering. It is shocking and upsetting to see how cruel women can be with their comments when they see another woman who happens to be beautiful. I think for instance of all of our brainwashed dictates on how we define beauty in our countries.

If we decide not to confirm to the typical given looks of beauty as mentioned previously we firmly take a stand against a form of violence. How many women have suffered terrible pains because of all these plastic surgeries that went wrong or subsequently created horrible side effects? I am not talking about simple fillers here but serious invasive procedures.

Why numerous women subject themselves to such scenarios? If these women would have a sense of profound connection with the real "I" they would categorically say no to putting their lives, health and safety at risk. This fact does not come from my personal opinion but is the testimony of dozens of actresses who were interviewed one day on a program about cosmetic procedures. One of them, a famous actress well known for her many procedures said that basically if this was to start all over again, she would simply stick to what Mother Nature had given her. She pursued saying that the pain she endured in the aftermath of her breast enlargement was excruciating like daggers in her back. This is a form of violence done on ourselves in the name of vanity. The sad part of it all is now younger and younger women subject themselves to all kinds of cosmetic procedures. We hardly hear about the nightmares from people who became victims of the aftermaths of procedures that went dire, leaving them with mental and physical scars.

I recently watched a TV talk show where a mother proudly announced that she had given breast implants for her daughter's sixteenth birthday. At sixteen years of age the body has not yet completed its growth. One can only wonder what will become of that girl when she turns sixty. Our society has adopted a new religion, a new cult called the infinite pursuit of physical perfection. There was a survey recently done in groups of girls ranging from 12 to 20 years of age. These girls were asked to describe what a physically perfect girl should look like. Eighty percent (70%) of these girls said that the ideal looking girl had to be tall, at least 5'6, slim with large breasts with long thick shiny hair and with glowing flawless skin. It appears that the "Barbie syndrome" is still very present in the psyche of young girls.

These high standards create a huge discrepancy between reality and illusion. As a result, many succumb to the desire to go under the knife knowing the dangers it entails. We should ask ourselves why we subject our bodies to violent changes and unnecessary physical pain. Could it be that we refuse to peacefully accept the fact that any "less than perfect" features will not stop others to love us or admire us for other beautiful qualities we have and give the world.

We have busy lives and the demands and pressures are such that we have a hard time coping with the required updates of our complex living. It does not look like it will get better since our lines of communications have become mostly "virtual" in our digital age. This situation isolates people further more from tangible reality. It deprives us from experiencing healthy natural human warmth. Will that phenomenon create a new race which will consist of grownups who will feel like neglected kids who don't belong in the big family? Only time will tell.

Many reports show an increasing number of kids suffering from unstable patterns of behavior. If these issues are not addressed at an early stage, it could lead to serious dysfunctions such as violence or aggressive acts. I hope we are not slowly denaturalizing the foundation of a nurturing society. Our family structures have exploded during the last three decades. We live in divorced and recomposed families in which meals are frequently spent with each family member glued on their cellular. These meals are not what it used to be like when the parents were there and the kids were sitting giving reports of their school day. I am not saying that these kind of family dynamics no longer exist but they are rare.

CHAPTER SIXTEEN

Practical Suggestions

Alright, I know you must think that it is enough philosophy and analytical observations for one day. Let's get down to business. I want to share the strategies I have developed over the years with my experience. They are practical suggestions and tricks I find helpful.

We are fortunate to live in an age where our options are multiple. With the internet, all necessary information is available. During my mother's days, the choices were extremely limited. I remember seeing two wigs in her closet. One was for her Bridge club and the other was to go out to dinner with my father. For her, they were fun accessories to play with. As for myself, after trials and tribulations and a few disasters and much wasted money, I have acquired easy ways to handle all possible situations that life offers on a daily basis.

The tricks depend on your individual capillary situation. If you have just started noticing a bit of loss of hair on your pillow or in the shower, you will want to see a hair specialist to assess the cause of your loss. Maybe it is due to a lack of minerals or stress. Do not panic since it will make the situation worse. There is always hope in any circumstances with the right solution. Believe me I have gone through my share of dramatic freak out sessions myself. My sleepless nights just aggravated the condition.

However, if you have passed this stage and are observing increasing amounts of patches, then the actual solution for that will be hair pieces or hair clips to fill these areas. The key to stop the anxiety which comes with hair loss is to have the right instruments at hand to minimize the visual consequences. Thus why it is essential to properly assess what is needed for your specific situation. I personally liked to have hair clips and hair pieces because they smoothly fit in my natural hair without noticing anything. It really helped me for a while and it decreased my level of fear. Remember there is a good solution for each phase of hair loss.

I took and went through each step, trying to remain calm and positive and felt grateful that whatever amount of hair I was losing, there was always a solution. The wigs I presently own are similar in shapes, length and colors. This way, it helps reducing in the overall costs of the accessories. If you have basically the same models, you do not have to replace them as frequently. I have three drawers. One drawer consists of the wigs I only wear when skiing, kickboxing, and going to the gym or doing yoga. These are easy to maintain and hold on very well on one's head. The fact that I have a few of these which I call my "outdoor" wigs, it does not require the high maintenance that my others do and it helps keeping them in good condition.

The second drawer consists of the ones I like to wear for nice occasions, dining out or meeting with friends. As I buy a new one, then the one which was the latest will give its place to the new wig. So at the end of the drawer I have the oldest wigs for these occasions. I have them all in zip lock bags and identified their purpose.

It goes without saying that the ones you will wear more often will definitely need to be washed accordingly. However, you do not want to wash them too often because eventually they will lose their luster and will no longer look natural. If you go in any hair salons where they sell extensions, weaving, and of course wigs, they will provide you with all essential shampoos and conditioners. They also will sell head forms on which you can pin the wig on after washing it so it can dry nicely. Remember that if you buy synthetic hair, you will not be able to blow dry the wig. If you prefer to display your wigs in your closet like some Hollywood actresses do, then that is fine. Make it easy and natural for yourself as possible. Again, as mentioned before, you will develop an easy routine that works best for you. I personally prefer to gently put my wigs in drawers to save space. I gently fold them nicely.

When I travel, I have two special little hard cases which look like jewelry holders in which I put the wigs in. The blue colored case is for the ones I wear for my outdoor activities and the brown case is for when I go out for dinner or shopping etc...

The bottom line is just be easy with whatever system you choose to adopt. We are fortunate now that we have hundreds of web sites to choose from. Hair pieces and wigs nowadays are beautifully made and look so natural.

Do your research and do your comparisons. There are many interesting websites. More and more actresses and models are launching their own brands of wigs. We have Beverly Johnson, Christy Brinkley, Raquel Welsh and Sheryl Tiegs to name just a few.

Trust your choices and do not buy them hastily or under any given pressure from the sales people. Buying a wig is not like buying a house but it is similar in its magnitude. The wig you will end up wearing will be like your second nature. It is an important expense. It is not a wig you buy to wear on Halloween night. You will wear it like a crown on your head which will make you feel good about yourself. I have a good friend of mine that recently told me that my alopecia served me well despite all the aggravations. It made me wear very glamorous hair styles throughout these last years with very little hassles along the way. The good news is I do not have to spend hundreds of dollars each month for haircut and hair coloring.

Conclusion

Whatever our challenges are in life, whether we have hair loss issues, weigh issues, whether we have addictions, weaknesses, mental blocks, or defeatist attitudes, we must decide whether we want to come out of these obstacles with our chin up and exude zest, passion and energy in our daily existence or cave in by giving up our power to these dysfunctions. I for myself have to admit that for a long period of time I settled comfortably in my own misery. It became an extension of myself and it took a proportion that overruled all other aspects of my life. For a while I could not imagine myself living happily and positively. I felt my life was like a train passing me by and I was not on that train.

My own breakthrough happened one night when I sank and drowned into the deepest despair and sadness. I caught myself sobbing nonstop and the more I was sobbing the more I was feeling sorry for myself. I almost died from the pain I felt in my heart due to that deep sorrow. I woke up the next day looking at myself straightforward in the mirror and saw these blue eyes of mine once filled with life and joy now were filled with sadness and swollen from the tears. I walked out of the bathroom and decided with all the inner strength and courage I had left in me that I would not end up living like that for the rest of my life. I no longer wanted to indulge myself in self-pity or misery. I wanted to embrace life with open arms. I wanted to be that woman on the Titanic in that movie where she is standing on the front deck of the boat, with her face in the wind breathing deeply the fragrance of the salt waters. Her arms are wide open as she embraces and welcomes the beauty of the vast ocean of life, that beautiful ocean given to all of us on earth.

Every day is a new start with new choices. I chose once and

for all to be grateful for what came from my individual experience. I do not see the glass half full or half empty, I am just happy to have a glass. I would lie to you if I said that it is easy. It is a workout in itself to re adjust all old beliefs, paradigms and all the little voices that for years tended to be more destructive. I have to learn to trust that life is like a puzzle and all the pieces of that big puzzle eventually fall into their proper place. Timing is an important factor in this relative life of ours. It seems that everything always come in its due time. In general, there is always a "breakdown" before the breakthrough.

Everyone has to decide what works best for themselves. We all have a path and we all have a purpose. Everyone is here for a specific reason. We all have talents, skills, abilities which need to be shared so we can help one another. We all have a place on this planet and whatever place that is, it is a special one because each and every one of us is unique. We have to choose in which camp we are going to live in. Will it be the camp where people are judged because how they look or will it be the camp where we are respected human beings for the amazing beauty we have inside which reflects through our eyes.

This book is my genuine way of extending my help to all of you. Let us remind ourselves that we all are work in progress and we all need to be more gentle and kinder with one another in order to allow the better of every one of us to be expressed. Let us leave the hardship of criticisms and condemnation behind and instead build our own wonderful beautiful new selves together. Let us heal together instead of letting our spiritual pride take over us.

Remember when you see a woman on the street and she is all decked out and you think she looks totally ridiculous, just keep in mind that she probably worked really hard to make herself pretty and at the end, the most important thing is that, in her eyes, she feels beautiful therefore she is. How we look does not define who we truly are.

I may be an idealist but at the end of the day it does not cost us anything by simply trying to live a life filled with more compassion and tolerance. Let's remember again and again that none of us are perfect and as long as we roll up our sleeves and keep trying, we will get there somehow, some day, I just know we will in the depth of my heart. One last thing, we do not need to be famous in order to have the power and the voice to help others.

REFERENCES:

"Human Physiology"
- Dr. Tony Nader

"Super Brain"
- Dr. Deepak Chopra and Rudolph Tanzi

"Destiny of Souls"
- Dr. Michael Newton

"Science of Being and Art of Living"
- Maharishi Mahesh Yogi

"A Course in Miracles"
- The Foundation for Inner Peace

www.ingramcontent.com/pod-product-compliance
Lightning Source LLC
Chambersburg PA
CBHW060131050426
42448CB00010B/2062